Mother of Broken India
Harbans Kaur

A biography of Harbans Kaur

(1913-1999)

By Dr Rupinder Singh

Supported by his brothers and sister

This Book is a companion volume of the Book entitled *Don't Break Up India* on martydom of her husband, Shaheed Sardar Nanak Singh, during the partition of India in 1947.

First published in Great Britain in 2018.

Copyright © Dr Rupinder Singh

The right of Dr Rupinder Singh to be identified as the Author has been asserted in accordance with the Copyright, Designs and Patents Act 1988.

Hardback ISBN: 978-0-85719-623-1

British Library Cataloguing in Publication Data
A CIP catalogue record for this book can be obtained from the British Library.

Produced and distributed by:
HARRIMAN HOUSE LTD
18 College Street, Petersfield, GU31 4AD
GREAT BRITAIN

DEDICATION

To women of the world who go through extreme hardships in the service of their family, community and country.

ACKNOWLEDGMENTS

Developing the biography of an extraordinary woman of India, Sardarni Harbans Kaur, has been a challenging adventure. She is no more in this world, her family is spread out across the globe and some key members of her family who were privy to many of the sufferings and challenges along the way, are also now not alive. Fortunately for me, I was lucky to have a very dedicated back up support team that helped me complete this historic project.

I would like to thank my eldest brother, Rajinder Singh, M.A., psc, for his valuable additions and reviews of the contents. Additionally, being a linguist, for his assistance in transforming my American English to Queen's English with meticulous attention to grammar. I am equally thankful to my youngest brother, Dr.Rami Ranger CBE, who encouraged me to embark upon this historic project - to describe the life of someone who will serve as a role model for women across the globe and inspire them to succeed in life under the most adverse circumstances. Every time we spoke, he would ask me "What is the progress on the book?" With this prod from him and others, I was able to maintain focus and momentum to complete the project.

My sister, Surinder Kaur Sahney, who is gifted with photographic memory, helped me place events in the correct chronological order and perspective and recollected names and places that had "evaporated" from my own memory. My younger brother, Devinder Singh, an army Colonel and an accomplished Electrical and Mechanical Engineer, did the impossible – as a self appointed custodian of family archives, he provided me with old newspaper cuttings, rare family photos and much other archived material. My younger brother, Kulvinder Singh, also an army Colonel and a gunner, encouraged me to remain focused to the end. My other younger brother Brijinder Singh, Wing Commander, Indian Air Force, had the longest stay with his mother, Sardarni Harbans Kaur, and shared many life events with her, unfortunately, we lost him in 1985. My brother Pritam Singh Rangar, always had a few words of wisdom to share. Once again, we lost him in 2009 and with that we lost the opportunity of sharing his recollections and experiences during the most stressful time of our mother's life.

I had an unwavering support of my wife, Gurcharan Jit Kaur, M.A., M.Ed. who reviewed the manuscript and offered many constructive suggestions for readability and content. I also had the unwavering support of Renu Ranger, wife of my youngest brother Rami Ranger, who improved the language and grammar throughout.

CONTENTS

TARLOCHAN SINGH
Ex-Member of Parliament
Former Chairman, National
Commission for Minorities, INDIA

सत्यमेव जयते

A-70, Mount Kailash,
East of Kailash, New Delhi - 110065
Phone : 011-29244664
E-mail : tarlochan@sansad.nic.in
tarlochan@tarlochansingh.com

FOREWORD
by Sardar Tarlochan Singh

It is believed that Sikhs rise from the ashes like a Phoenix and by sheer faith in Satguru they not only survive but make notable achievements. Guru Gobind Singh, prophet of optimism has made every follower remain optimistic. I am happy to be associated with this book which is a story of the courage of a widow who by her efforts raised her family after being uprooted from Pakistan. I am happy to recall that I had the privilege of knowing her, as one of her sons was my classmate in Mahindra College, Patiala.

The book in your hands is truly motivational. It exemplifies the human capacity for endurance and determination for survival when drowning in fathomless adversities. It narrates the true life struggle for survival of a newly widowed mother with eight children in the calamity of India's partition in 1947. This partition was neither peaceful nor organised. No one ever foresaw the "rivers of blood" that would flow. Sadly, it happened amidst total anarchy and mayhem, with mass murder, rape and the destruction of property becoming commonplace.

The unprecedented exodus of millions of people took place on religious grounds from one part of Punjab to safe havens in other parts several hundred miles apart. The desperate people formed human caravans, on foot, bullock carts and other means of transportation, with whatever little they could carry whilst fleeing. On the way, many of these caravans were intercepted by religious fanatics — causing more destruction, death and untold sufferings. I can very well recall these tragic incidents as I was one of those migrants who were uprooted from Pakistan.

Having been uprooted from Multan, a penniless Harbans Kaur with her eight children arrived in the Princely State of Patiala. With courage and determination, she envisioned her challenges for a place to live, some means of income and education for her children. She frantically searched for kind-hearted people who could guide and support her in her ordeal.

Being actively engaged in the social and political affairs of Patiala and surrounding communities, it was my good fortune to have met Harbans Kaur on several occasions and to appreciate the challenges she faced whilst dealing with the maze of bureaucracy in order to identify opportunities to further her determined settlement. I also realised that she was helping other women who were less fortunate than her to face and overcome the challenges of survival during those extremely unpredictable times.

The book narrates the true events of her life and how she translated these challenges into a phenomenal success story of her remarkable achievements.

I am confident that this book will lift the spirits of its readers and provide an insight into how the most difficult challenges of life might be overcome. It is the story of an unimaginable achievement by a young widow with overwhelming responsibilities.

Tarlochan Singh

Sadar Tarlochan Singh
Ex-MP
Former Chairman, National Commission for Minorities
Govt. of India
August 2017

CHAPTER I:
Pre-Partition Punjab 1947, India

Harban Kaur's life began and revolved within the Province of Punjab before the partition of India in 1947. Punjab had been under Muslim rule until Maharaja Ranjit Singh defeated the Mogul armies and established a Sikh kingdom in 1799 with the capital at Lahore. After almost 50 years, the British annexed Punjab in 1849 by defeating the Sikh armies in the Anglo-Sikh Wars of 1845 and 1849. Punjab along with the rest of India came under the British rule (Raj) which lasted until 1947.

Maharaja Ranjit Singh
(1780-1839)

Map of India with the Empire
of Maharaja Ranjit Singh
shown in red

The word "Punjab" is made of two words Punj (Five) + Aab (Water) i.e. the land of five rivers. It was named as such because five rivers flowed through this land. They are the Sutlej, Beas, Ravi, Chenab and Jhelum and these five rivers are tributaries of the Indus River which then merge into the Indus directly or indirectly. The Indus River itself terminates in the Arabian Sea near the port city of Karachi which is now in Pakistan.

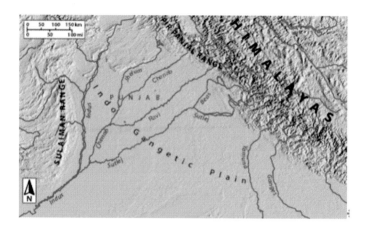

The Five Rivers of Punjab - (Sutlej, Beas, Ravi, Chenab and Jhelum merge into River Indus)

The geographical alignment of the rivers managed to create remarkable cultural identities for all the inhabitants within their boundaries. These were identified as below:

Doaba: The area between the rivers of Beas and Sutlej. The major cities within this area are Jalandhar, Hoshiarpur and Nawan Shahar.

Majha: The area between the rivers of Beas and Chenab. The major cities are Lahore, Gujranwala, Amritsar, Gurdaspur, Sialkote, Kasur, Fridkot, Ferozepur, Lyallpur (Faisalabad), Montgomery (Saiwal).

Malwa: The area of Malwa is southern Punjab, facing Rajasthan and East of the Beas River. The major cities are Ludhiana, Patiala, Ambala, Karnal, Sangrur, Malerkotla, Shahabad, and Abohar.

Pothohar: This was the area beyond the Chenab river in the North and around west of the Jhelum river. The major cities included Rawalpindi and Hasan Abdal (Punja Sahib).

Punjab with its five rivers was one of the most fertile regions of India and was ideal for growing wheat, rice, sugar cane, fruits and vegetables. It also produced a sizeable portion of cotton, barley and maize. It was called the "Bread Basket of India" and the economy of the State was predominantly based on agriculture – around 85% by some estimates.

Punjab has her roots in one of the oldest civilisations on earth with a distinguished language, culture, food, attire, script and folklore. The Punjabi language was, and still is, spoken across Punjab with varying dialects.

Given this background, one can imagine Sardarni Harban Kaur's early life in the Punjab. After her marriage, she moved to different locations within the Punjab Province accompanying her husband during his frequent postings whilst serving in the British Punjab Police.

CHAPTER II:
Growing Up

Harbans Kaur was born on 15th March 1913 in the village of Khokharkee, District Gujranwala, in the Province of Punjab which became part of the Pakistani Punjab after Partition of India in 1947. She was the third of ten children in the family of father, Sardar Kesar Singh and mother Sardarni Ishar Kaur. Her parents owned several acres of farming land in the village and her mother was a devoted housewife taking care of the large family of five sons and five daughters.

"I remember my golden childhood. In the house of my parents it was a blissful period of security, joy and happiness. It was like paradise. I had no care in the world. All the year round we had plenty of food, milk and butter. There were maids at home, workers in dad's farms and 'tongas' (horse drawn carriages) and riding horses to go around. I was so much spoilt that all used to call me 'Malika' (Queen)."

Right from her childhood Sardarni Harbans Kaur's parents taught her to love and respect Gurbani, the utterances and compositions of the Sikh Gurus and the Sikh Holy Scriptures. They were devout Sikhs who lived their lives according to the teachings of the Gurus.

Her father used to get up at the crack of dawn, take a bath and then say prayers and meditate on divine consciousness. At prayer time in the mornings, her father used to call all the children to join in the prayers. Gradually, the teachings of the Gurus began to have an impact on Harbans Kaur and she started to understand God's message of humility, devotion and care and concern for the others. Her mother would say her prayers and start preparing nourishing meals for the large family.

One morning Harbans Kaur took the firm pledge not to start her day or eat anything without saying her prayers. She used to recite Japji Sahib daily before eating anything. Traditionally, Sikh hymns from the Holy Scriptures are recited by singing. Along with her gifted voice, she learnt to play the Harmonium as an accompaniment. As she developed her musical skills, she also developed a flair for public speaking on religious, family and social themes, interpreting the word of Sikh Gurus. She became a staunch devotee of Guru Nanak Dev, the first Guru and the founder of Sikh religion. God's Will was so powerful and benign towards her that later her husband's name was also Nanak Singh.

At the time of her birth and while she was growing up, India was a British colony and had remained so from 1776 until 1947. India was an agrarian country with over 90% of her population living in villages, indulging predominantly in farming, agriculture and dairy. Education systems at primary and secondary levels were confined to urban centres only. Educational opportunities for girls were limited, even though Sikh girls had no social or religious restrictions. Equality for women has been enshrined in the Sikh religion ever since the founding of the religion over 560 year ago.

As progressive parents, they enrolled their daughter in a school a few miles away in the District City of Gujranwala. Her parents met a teacher, named Mayavanti, at the Khalsa Middle School and trusted her with the care of their child. This kind hearted teacher would often take her to the nearby Mandir (Temple). The deities of Hanuman and other gods and goddesses were installed in a dark room. She used to be scared and would tightly hold on to the teacher's finger. The 'Pujari' (priest), would place a 'tilak tikka' (vermillion mark) on her forehead and would pour a spoon full of 'tulsi' water (consecrated water) on her hands to drink. The 'Pujari' would also give her a 'patasa' (candy bubble).

Whenever her parents' came to collect her from the school, they would bring milk, butter, ghee (purified butter), vegetables and whole-wheat flour for the teacher. The teacher was very happy with this arrangement and took good care of little Harbans. During weekends, the family tonga (horse driven buggy) would take her to her parents house and bring her back to school in comfort.

Her parents were very happy to see their daughter complete her early schooling successfully. This was a tremendous achievement considering the poor educational standards of women and girls in those days. Overall, the rate of illiteracy in India was at an all-time high of around 85%.

The large family was comprised of ten children. Five sons: Havela Singh, Mela Singh, Faujdar Singh, Hazara Singh and Sardar Singh and five daughters: Sant Kaur, Harbans Kaur, Sharan Kaur, Piar Kaur and Mohinder Kaur, in that order. The first name of Sikh boys and men as well as girls and women can be the same. The last name or surname is constantly "Singh" for boys and men. Likewise, the last name or surname for girls and women invariably ends in "Kaur." This can sometimes be confusing to the others not familiar with the Sikh naming system.

On completion of her basic education, Harbans Kaur came back to her village to live with her parents and siblings. She was a great help to her mother in taking care of her younger brothers and sisters and assisted her mother in many of the household activities such as decorating, attending to visitors and looking after the guests, and so on.

One may like to imagine the life of a family in those yonder years with the absence of the modern amenities that we are so used to in the twenty-first century. Telephones were very scarce. The All India Radio was only established in 1936, black and white television did not make its debut until the 1960s. Words like the Internet, computers and mobile phones were not found in any dictionary. One wonders then how the children managed to entertain themselves and make social contacts. Surprisingly enough, the children in fact had many avenues to maintain their social and peer to peer contacts in those days by indulging in a variety of outdoor activities. The boys would play marbles, field hockey, 'Pithu' and soccer; accompany their elders on long walks, hunting expeditions, farming activities and help in taking care of the livestock, etc. Girls like Harbans Kaur, would be involved in domestic chores such as cooking, knitting and sewing. The girls also engaged in cultural activities, they played folklore games such as 'giddha,' 'shitapu,' 'chicho chich ganerian,' 'Lukan Miti' (hide and seek) short skits and the like. It was fun all round. Harbans Kaur always nurtured happy memories of those care-free childhood days.

Kikli

Giddha

CHAPTER III:
Married Life

Time flies, as they say. It was the year 1931 when Harbans Kaur turned 18. Her parents assumed the traditional responsibility of finding a suitable life partner for her. The process of an arranged marriage has been an integral part of the Indian culture for generations. A marriage is termed as 'arranged' when it is arranged by people other than those getting married. Most often, the other people involved in the arrangement of the marriage are the parents of the boys and girls. The parents or relatives effectively act as sponsors, taking responsibility to get the boy or girl married to a good partner. This process curtails the phenomenon of courtship as we understand these days. It is believed that 95% of all current Indian marriages are arranged, either through family or friends. The success rate of arranged marriages is still very high in India even these days.

Living in a small village of Khokharkee, a few miles from the district town of Gujranwala, the social circle of Harbans Kaur's parents was somewhat limited. It occurred to them to go to Lahore, the capital of the Punjab, and place a matrimonial advertisement in one of the leading dailies of the Province. This thought prophetically turned out to be a good one. The editor of the newspaper, while taking down the write-up on Harbans, informed them that there was a Sikh family sitting in the next room who had just finished submitting a write-up seeking a suitable bride for their son. This was an unexpected coincidence. Sardar Kesar Singh and Sardarni Ishar Kaur introduced themselves to Dr Wazir Singh and his wife Sardarni Jeevan Kaur, the parents of the boy. They told them that their son had studied at the prestigious Forman Christian College (FC College), and had graduated with the degree of B.Sc. (Hons) from

Panjab University and had subsequently completed a law degree from Law College, Lahore. Their son had been selected by the Punjab police as a prosecuting inspector and had recently completed his training at the Punjab police academy at Philaur in Punjab. Presently, he was posted at Sargodha, a district town of Punjab. After an exchange of pleasantries, the two families struck a common chord and decided to pursue the matrimonial matters further.

After a few months of correspondence, the parents decided to introduce their children to each other. It was decided to meet in Rawalpindi where the boy's parents lived and owned ancestral properties. Dr Wazir Singh was posted as a Civil Surgeon in the local hospital. Everything fell into place in 1931 and the marriage was solemnised according to Sikh rites in Lahore.

Newly Married Harbans Kaur and Nanak Singh

As part of a daily routine, Sardarni Harbans Kaur (also now known as Mrs Nanak Singh) used to get up in the early morning and recite gurbani from memory. Her father-in-law and mother-in-law would join in the prayers. Her father-in-law was well versed in gurbani and would provide minor corrections during her recitation. He would also provide a brief interpretation of the meanings in common language. He would often mention to her mother-in-law that their house had become a paradise with the arrival of their daughter-in-law who was so much immersed in the Sikh faith and religion. Harbans Kaur could recite substantial portions of the Sikh holy book, Sri Guru Granth Sahib, from memory.

Harbans Kaur's husband, being in service with the Punjab police as a prosecuting inspector, was frequently moved from place to place within the province of Punjab. Among the many towns of his tenures were Kartarpur, Alipore, Leiah, Jhelum, Multan, Khanewal, Rawalpindi, Pind Dadan Khan, Mian Channu, and Sargodha.

Subsequently, Sardar Nanak Singh's postings to the difficult stations of Rajanpur, Jampur and Dera Ghazi Khan were necessitated as a punishment for his refusal to open fire to disperse a peaceful demonstration in Sargodha where they were demanding independence from the British rule. These particular police stations were across the mighty Indus River from the ferry port at Muzafargarh, West of Multan. Obeying these orders, the family moved from Sargodha to Multan and onwards to Rajanpur. The River Indus in those early days had no road bridge and the banks of the river were over two miles apart. The family crossed the River Indus by a steam powered ferry that was invariably loaded with camels, goats, fat-tailed sheep and a host of other provisions for the tribal population on the other side of the river. It was always an arduous journey.

On reaching the far bank of the river, the family boarded a lorry to take them to Rajanpur over bumpy roads. Rajanpur was a small town in the far south western part of the Punjab region which at that time had a small population.

Steam powered ferry

On reaching Rajanpur, Sardarni Harbans Kaur found herself in a strange and isolated environment. The majority of the tribal population in this remote and isolated region were Muslims with strong ties to the culture of the neighbouring province of Balochistan to the west. Almost all of the women in the area were illiterate.

From Rajanpur, the next posting was to Jampur, another small town a few miles away. After that, Sardar Nanak Singh and his family were shunted out to Dera Ghazi Khan, a district headquarters of these townships.

Sardarni Harbans Kaur saw a window of opportunity to interact with the tribal women and encourage them to seek the light of knowledge through literacy. With this aim in mind, Sardarni Harbans Kaur immediately became involved in community service and started an adult education centre for the women of Rajanpur and then Jampur. Word of her volunteer adult education reached Miss Caleb, the District Inspectress of Schools at Dera Ghazi Khan, who made a visit to Rajanpur to see for herself the education activity under her jurisdiction. The initial class strength had increased from 18 women students to 25 students. Besides there were an additional 22 girl students attending the evening class. The news of Harbans Kaur's efforts in bringing literacy to the women and girls in the community was widely written about. On returning to her office, Miss Caleb sent two letters of appreciation dated 3 February 1943 and 23 June 1943 to Sardarni Harbans Kaur, appreciating her efforts in promoting adult education, as follows:

Office of the District Inspectress of Schools, Dera Ghazi Khan, dated 3rd. February, 1943.

It has been a great pleasure to see Mrs. Nanak Singh's Gurmukhi class at her residence. The most encouraging feature of this class is 18 women who have learnt to read and write in less than two months' time. This shows Mrs. Nanak Singh is taking a keen interest in the adult literacy work and is helping her illiterate sisters to become literate. I wish her every success in this noble undertaking.

I will be pleased to have a report of her work every month. The particulars of those adults who can read and write well should be sent to my office for issuing certificates to them.

Sd. A.B. Caleb, District Inspectorate of Schools, Dera Ghazi Khan.

Office of the District Inspectress of Schools, Dera Ghazi Khan, dated 23rd June, 1943.

Dear Mrs. Nanak Singh,

It gave me much pleasure to examine your adult class and to give out literacy certificates to the 10 who had already finished their course. I do hope the number of adults will still increase.

I was also pleased to note that besides these 25 adults there were 22 girls who were attending the evening class regularly and had achieved so much in this short time.

This shows how keen you are to serve humanity. I appreciate your good work and wish you success in your undertakings in this connection.

Yours sincerely,

Sd. A.B. Caleb, District Inspectress of Schools, Dera Ghazi Khan.

Meanwhile, Sardar Nanak Singh had realised that the British government had cleverly sidelined him away from the mainstream independence movement for which he had a great zeal and passion. So, he took the bold decision to resign from the police service so that he would be able to do what was necessary to support the independence movement. This was a momentous decision for the family since Sardar Nanak Singh had an outstanding service career with over twenty police meritorious commendation certificates and a secure employment.

After his resignation, the family moved to Multan where Sardar Nanak Singh established his law practice, being a well-qualified attorney. One might ask as to why Sardar Nanak Singh chose to settle down in Multan. He could have established his law practice in Lahore, the capital of Punjab province, or in Rawalpindi itself at his ancestral birth place. His parents, Dr. Wazir Singh and Sardarni Jeevan Kaur, had four residential properties in Rawalpindi and large tracts of agricultural lands in the village of Kuntrila in the Rawalpindi district. However, Sardar Nanak Singh chose to establish his law practice in Multan since he knew the area well, having served there earlier as prosecuting inspector with the Punjab police. He also had a great deal of personal contacts in Multan that would help him to establish and grow his law practice. Multan had a population of just 2 to 3% Hindus and Sikhs in an otherwise predominantly Muslim region. The non-Muslim population mostly comprised of professionals and those in business.

Most importantly, being in his own private practice offered Sardar Nanak Singh endless opportunities to focus on his passion – to mobilise public opinion to put an end to the British Raj in India. Sardarni Harbans Kaur always supported her husband in his political activities for India's freedom. Many delegates would drop by for meetings and discussions. They were always treated as honoured guests and provided with food and occasionally with makeshift accommodation.

Once settled in this new place, Multan, Sardarni Harbans Kaur involved herself with the community and the children soon became immersed in their education.

CHAPTER IV:
The Year of Change 1947

World War II had just been won in 1945 by the Allied forces and the War had left Britain short of manpower and resources to govern her vast colonies in all parts of the world. At the same time there was growing unrest in the British colonies. In India the freedom movement was gaining ground. The Indian political leaders such as Mohandas Karamchand Gandhi and Pandit Jawaharlal Nehru of the All-India Congress Party raised their voices louder, demanding independence. On the other side, the All India Muslim League, had set their eyes on the partition of India in order to carve out a purely Islamic nation, Pakistan, meaning Land of the Pure!

The Presidential address by Muhammad Ali Jinnah to the All-India Muslim League in Lahore, 1940 contained the following passage summarizing the political mood of the time:

"But one thing is quite clear: it has always been taken for granted mistakenly that the Mussalmans are a minority, and of course we have got used to it for such a long time that these settled notions sometimes are very difficult to remove. The Mussalmans are not a minority. The Mussalmans are a nation by any definition. The British and particularly the All-India Congress Party proceed on the basis, "Well, you are a minority after all, what do you want!" "What else do the minorities want?" just as Babu Rajendra Prasad said. But surely the Mussalmans are not a minority. We find that even according to the British map of India we occupy large parts of this country where the Mussalmans are in a majority, such as Bengal, Punjab, N.W.F.P., Sind, and Balochistan."

Address by Quaid-i-Azam Mohammad Ali Jinnah at Lahore Session of Muslim League, March 1940 (Islamabad: Directorate of Films and Publishing, Ministry of Information and Broadcasting, Government of Pakistan, Islamabad, 1983, pp. 5-23)

The mindset of the Muslim population was continuously prepared to aspire for a separate country where they would hold a majority. If this was done then the other communities would by default, become minorities interspersed all over Pakistan. It was therefore resolved by the All-India Muslim League to expel the minorities from areas where the Muslim were already in majority. Minorities in these areas, particularly the Sikhs and the Hindus in Punjab who had lived and flourished there for centuries had to relocate themselves in very adverse conditions to the non-Muslim majority areas elsewhere in India. The obvious intention was to force out the minorities from the Muslim majority areas by creating a sense of insecurity and panic amongst them. During this time, abduction, looting, rape and massacres were carried out on a widespread basis. Apparently, the leadership of the All-India Congress Party had no vision or plan and they were caught ill prepared and by complete surprise.

On March 3, 1947, the news came of the fall of the Government in Punjab amidst public agitation and protests against the break-up of India solely on the basis of religion. On this day, Master Tara Singh, leader of the Sikhs, held a large rally along with some 500 of his Sikhs supporters. Climbing up the Punjab Legislative Assembly building in Lahore, he tore up the flag of Pakistan that some Muslim miscreants had hoisted earlier, and declared 'Death to Pakistan!' At this time, the mob of about 50,000 Muslims outside went berserk. Master Tara Singh and his loyal Sikh followers narrowly avoided a violent clash with the pro Pakistani Muslims.

In the city of Multan Sardar Nanak Singh, President of the District Minorities Federation, along with Dr. Saifuddin Kitchlew, a senior Congress leader, called a rally of all citizens on March 4, 1947 at Kup Maidan, to protest against the establishment of Pakistan, a fundamentalist Islamic State. They could foresee the destruction and devastation of the Land of Five Rivers (Punjab) if communities turned against each other on the basis of religion. This rally was well attended with speaker after speaker cautioning against the mutilation of India in such a crude manner that would pose a serious threat to inter-religious harmony and social equilibrium in India. The air was now charged with tension, waiting for an explosion.

Sardar Nanak Singh called upon the people to remain united and peaceful and he took up a firm stand against the Partition of India. In his address he repeated Mahatma Gandhi's call to keep India united "Akhand Bharat".

On this very day, wide scale rioting suddenly erupted in Multan, Lahore and the adjoining areas. As Jinnah had declared "Muslims are no believers in non-violence", each Muslim tried to prove this point by plundering, pillaging, abducting, raping, murdering and engaging in other despicable acts of savagery. This exasperated the communal situation, increasing the animosity between the Sikhs and the Hindus on one side, and the Muslims on the other.

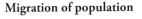

Migration of population   **Migration by bullock carts**

Panic stricken refugees began moving to safety by all means available

Dead bodies strewn across streets

The next day, 5th of March, 1947, life appeared to have returned to normal in Multan. Sardar Nanak Singh went to court to take care of the legal cases in progress. His wife, Sardarni Harbans Kaur, sent the children off to school and engaged in household chores. At about 10 o'clock in the morning, students of DAV High School came out of their classes to demonstrate against the break-up of India. As they marched towards the city, pupils from the nearby locality started to join those shouting slogans against the formation of Pakistan.

As everyone had feared, the children while passing through the streets were attacked by the pro-Pakistan mob armed with sticks, machetes and knives. There were many wounded, and bleeding children crying in pain and agony. This awful news reached the Judicial Court where Sardar Nanak Singh was busy defending a client. He immediately stopped his work and rushed to the scene of the attack.

Ignoring the sincere advice of several of his colleagues, Sardar Nanak Singh left the judicial court and reached the city centre known as Bohrh Darwaza (Gate) where he saw the ghastly scene of badly wounded school children writhing in pain and agony and crying for help. Around them were abandoned school bags, shoes and items of clothing belonging to them. The unarmed students were surrounded by these merciless attackers and were trapped thus making it difficult for them to escape. Some who managed to get away were being chased and those who could not run fast enough were set upon and severely injured. Sardar Nanak Singh shouted, "Stop attacking children. Stop it! What are you doing? Have some consideration for their tender age. These are unarmed schoolchildren, just shouting slogans". He addressed the killers with utmost courage: "Do not raise your hands on these innocent children."

But no one listened to him and turned on him instead shouting that he was the enemy of Pakistan. "Let us kill him, kill him," they chanted.

Within seconds Sardar Nanak Singh found himself surrounded by these men who attacked him with rage and fury. They inflicted 11 deep cuts in his skull and he succumbed to these grievous wounds and attained immortality through martyrdom. Fortunately before falling, he managed to rescue many innocent children from the claws of death by diverting their attackers fury towards himself and making way for the 600-700 Hindu-Sikh school children to escape from the murderous pro-Pakistan fanatical attack.

From then on, a life of superhuman challenges and untold sufferings and hardships befell Sardarni Harbans Kaur thereafter. She found herself suddenly plunged into a blood soaked series of events that broke up the country seemingly with the force of a thousand nuclear bombs, causing horrendous massacres and unparalleled mass migration across the sub-continent.

The first concern of the Hindu Sewa Samithi, a charity organization in Multan, was for the safety of Sardarni Harbans Kaur and her children. Very shortly, a car pulled up in front of her house on Kutchery Road, Multan, the driver explained to Sardarni Harbans Kaur the urgent need to quickly leave the house as a mob was moving towards the home to annihilate the entire family. He urged her to leave immediately; time was of the essence.

Sardarni Harbans Kaur quickly assembled her children and hurriedly organized an emergency exit from their home and the family was taken to a safer place – a family friend's house in the cantonment area.

At that time, her eldest son, Rajinder, was barely 15 years old. The other five sons and one daughter each had a two year age difference between them. The youngest child, Brijinder, was only 2 years old and Raminder, the seventh son, was not to see his father. He was born posthumously three months later. But destiny is supreme and cannot be averted.

The news of Sardar Nanak Singh's assassination was eventually conveyed to Sardarni Harbans Kaur. For her, this day of March 5, 1947, became the day of the Holocaust as her husband, a prominent political leader and an illustrious legal scholar, was assassinated. Her life as a life partner in raising the family and supporting her husband in his political struggle for the country's independence suddenly and abruptly came to an end. Overnight her children were left fatherless and she became a widow without a bread winner. Her own life was thus suddenly plunged into pitch darkness.

With utmost courage and by overcoming her immense personal grief, Sardarni Kaur, began rationalising her future course of action for survival. The first task before her was to organize a proper funeral for her husband whose body, covered with a white sheet, was lying in the morgue at Multan. Because of his head injuries, his head and face were wrapped in white bandages which was very distressing for her and her children to see.

Sardar Nanak Singh's paternal uncle, Dr. Sahib Singh, a medical doctor, was posted at Mian Channu, approximately 100 kilometres north east of Multan and this was approximately two hours' drive away. Another option was to take the body to Rawalpindi, to his parental home, where her father-in law, Dr. Wazir Singh, a Civil Surgeon, lived with his wife, Sardarni Jeevan Kaur. Rawalpindi was at a distance of approximately 560 kilometres which would take the family six to seven hours to reach by road.

Since Rawalpindi was already engulfed in violent attacks on Sikhs and Hindus it was not considered a safe place to go to. So, Sardarni Harbans Kaur decided to go to Mian Channu for the cremation. Dr Sahib Singh and his family, offered their utmost support to the grieving family, and she along with her children stayed there for a few extra days after the cremation.

Where should I go next? Many thoughts crossed her mind. Finally, she decided to take the family to Gujranwala a town which was about 10 miles away from her parents' village of Khokharkee.

Travelling by train, the family reached Gujranwala in early April 1947. At Gujranwala she was received with her children by the famous philanthropist, Bawa Harkishan Singh, Principal of Khalsa College. He and his wife Lakshman Kaur had a house in Guru Nanak Pura. They were a blessed couple living the noble way of life. They welcomed the distressed family into their own home with open arms. Sardarni Harbans Kaur's youngest child, Raminder, was born under the care and attention of the host family.

However, during June 1947 riots broke out in the city and there were numerous murders of Hindus and Sikhs who ventured out of their homes.

There were constant army patrols in trucks and jeeps attempting to keep order in the city. Only a few people doing essential jobs were given the permits to move about during curfew hours when everybody else had to be indoors. Bawa Harkishan Singh being in a prominent position had the permit. So he very kindly used to bring milk, bread and vegetables for Sardarni Harbans Kaur and her children every day. A few days after the birth of Raminder, a house for the family was found in nearby Gobind Garh colony where Sardarni Harbans Kaur and her children were moved to House Number 2. This house was owned by a businessman from Bangkok who was in hurry to go back and he let the house on rent of Rs.40 per month. Bawa Harkishan Singh paid the deposit of Rs. 400 which was the advance rent for ten months. The closeness of this house to the residence of Principal Bawa Harkishan Singh soon proved to be a blessing for the survival of the uprooted distressed family.

From June 1947 onwards Gujranwala, too, was engulfed in bloody riots. As the communal situation was deteriorating rapidly, Sardarni Harbans Kaur, decided that it was time to move across the anticipated Pakistan border to India.

For Sardarni Harbans Kaur this was the only choice to relative safety, there was no other way to escape. With a sinking heart she took this difficult decision, having seen her little children become deprived of their father's care, love and protection. She constantly prayed to God for strength and tried to link her mind with the perception of God's presence through "simran" that is reciting verses from the Sikh Holy Book. She used to pray, "O God, I cannot control my mind. It is restless and it is sinking in depression all the time." The inner voice would answer, "Your grandfather, Sardar Labh Singh, had joined the holy men ("sadhus") to pray. But you being a woman should go to Satsang (congregation in gurdwara) in order to concentrate your mind on Gurbani and thus comfort your troubled soul."

Only a few days after Sardarni Harbans Kaur had decided to move, the Baloch military was deployed in the City of Gujranwala. They started firing indiscriminately into areas inhabited by Hindus and Sikhs. There was great panic all around. People started leaving their homes in order to save their dear lives. The sounds of the gun shots could be heard intermittently throughout the day and night. Bullets came through windows and killed people indiscriminately. It did not seem at that time that God was protecting the weak or the innocent.

Curfews were enforced even more vigorously and over longer periods of time. Anyone going out to buy food was shot dead on the spot. Soon the riots overtook the village of Khokharkee where her parents lived thus making any help from her parents impossible. Her Saviour once again was Bawa Harkishan Singh who along with his two friends, Rann Singh and Niranjan Singh helped. They too had to obtain passes issued by the government which enabled them to go through the dangerous deserted streets during curfew hours to buy groceries and other essentials.

There was an eerie uncertainty about the future of Gujranwala. The Redcliff Report on the partition of India was expected within a few months. It was obvious that if Gujranwala was awarded to Pakistan, the non-Muslim population would suffer enormous losses in the form of human lives and properties. At that time the rail and road network would not have had sufficient capacity to handle the massive population movement. Sardarni Harbans Kaur thought of going to Ferozepur where her younger brother, Sardar Faujdar Singh, lived with his young family. Ferozepur was further east of the expected boundary line since it had a majority Hindu Sikh population. She took the decision to move out of Gujranwala in July 1947 – just in time before the situation deteriorated further, which would have made escape virtually impossible.

Her younger brother Sardar Faujdar Singh and his wife Sardarni Harbhajan Kaur were at that time living in Ferozepur Cantonment and they beseached Sardarni Harbans Kaur to move to their residence immediately, prior to the announcement of the Boundary Commission as Gujranwala was anticipated to be awarded to Pakistan. This was a God sent offer. Sardarni Harbans Kaur with eight of her children immediately moved to her brother's house in Ferozepur Cantonment. In the meantime Sardar Faujdar Singh spotted a house just vacated by a Muslim family. He immediately took possession of the house and Sardarni Harbans Kaur and her children moved into the house. It was a great relief to the family.

The City of Ferozepur is near Hussainiwala Head Works that was built under the Sutlej Valley project in 1926 in order to harness and regulate the waters of River Ravi and its tributary River Beas. Even though the move to Ferozepur was well thought out, it was not permanent. The heavy monsoon rains during August-September 1947 raised the level of water at the Headworks and the enormous overflow of water of the rivers led to severe flooding that deluged the City of Ferozepur and the adjoining areas. Once again, there was panic all around and the residents began evacuating to safer locations.

"Where will I go now with eight children?" This scary question kept going round and round in Sardarni Harbans Kaur's troubled mind. She thought of her younger sister, Sardarni Mohinder Kaur and her brother-in-law Sardar Shamsher Singh who lived in the Sikh princely State of Patiala.

But first she had to get away from the rising waters as all means of public transportation were already overbooked and she could not find a way to leave the deluged city of Ferozepur. There was no way of finding any means of transportation. Being always optimistic and her faith in God intact, she packed up her meagre belongings and waited for some sort of miracle transport. She stood by the roadside with tears in her eyes and prayed to God Almighty to come to her aid.

Sure enough, God answered her prayers. At the very moment a miracle happened. She saw a "tonga", a one horse carriage, coming straight towards her ignoring all the other people who were in line and wanted to hire it. When the "tonga" stopped near her, many distressed people left the queue and gathered around the "tonga" clamouring to hire it. But the kind hearted driver stood firm and said, "I have come only for this woman in distress with small children."

Sardarni Harbans Kaur was overcome with the kindness of the man and was greatly relieved of her worries by an unexpected gesture by this kind man and thankfully hired the "tonga" for travel to Faridkot, a distance of 33 km. After about four to five hours of a long, bumpy and weary ride, the family eventually disembarked at Faridkot railway station where they learnt that a refugee train headed for Patiala would be arriving in approximately seven to eight hours, this was a blessing in itself. Many people were already waiting at the platform. Leaving the children at the platform, Sardarni Harbans Kaur went in search for food for them. She reached the town and purchased few essential groceries from the nearby shops and cooked simple meals on an improvised makeshift fire at the railway platform and fed her hungry children. While sprawled on the ground in front of the station at Faridkot, once again God reached out to her. A one time neighbour, Sardar Ram Singh, happened to be the Station Master. He recognised her and took her to his quarters nearby. His wife prepared food for the family. The fatigued family rested a while in his house while waiting for the train to arrive.

Finally, when the train arrived, the waiting sea of displaced humanity rushed to enter the train compartments. It was a chaotic and desperate melee and only the fittest and the young could get into the train compartments, many being pushed through the windows. The rest began to perch on the roof top of the train. Sardarni Harbans Kaur, surrounded by her young and exhausted children, was bewildered and stood motionless in a helpless state on the railway platform. In the confusion and rush of refugees, her two year old son, Brijinder Singh, went missing. She became hysterical and she refused to move until her child was found. Her 15-year old son eldest son Rajinder searched frantically for his younger brother and with the grace of God, found him in the crowd a short distance away. In the meantime, the engine driver blew the whistle indicating that the overloaded train was about to leave. After a short while the train with overflowing passengers started moving leaving behind helpless Sardarni Harbans Kaur with her children. Luckily, this situation caught the attention of the kind hearted engine driver. When the long overflowing train was already pulling away, he applied the brakes and stopped the train, asking Sardarni Harbans Kaur if she and her children would board the locomotive itself since there was no other option. The chances of another train coming along was highly unlikely in the foreseeable future so she gratefully accepted the offer. The children climbed up and parked themselves on the engine tender which was loaded with coal for the steam locomotive.

Along the way the train stopped at some small stations, many of which were deserted given the traumatic times being faced by all. At some stations, local villagers would bring food and water to the unfortunate refugees who were fleeing for their lives. The trains were few and far between and were running very slowly. It was understood that all passengers were without tickets.

The Journey to Patiala was a distance of 187 km and the journey took about four or five long hours. The passengers all heaved a sigh of relief when the train eventually reached Patiala without any major incidences.

Sardarni Harbans Kaur and her children were received by her youngest sister Sardarni Mohinder Kaur and brother-in-law Sardar Shamsher Singh who were waiting at the railway station. Sardarni Harbans Kaur and her children stayed with them for about a month before moving into a deserted house in Gali Saifan Wali in Mohalla Mir Kundla which had been vacated by a wealthy Muslim merchant and his family who had migrated to Karachi, now in Pakistan.

In the ongoing violent political whirlwind all her relatives and friends had been uprooted and scattered across the country. People had been made homeless overnight and were fleeing as refugees in all directions seeking a safe place to live. Tragically during this time hundreds of millions of people were affected and suffered, losing all of their possessions. Law and order had now completely broken down, there were no welfare offices to turn to and the administration was in complete disarray. During this time, the thought of saving one's home and hearth was inconceivable, coupled with the fact that the police and military units themselves were in utter chaos, with loyalties changing rapidly to either secular India or the Islamic Republic of Pakistan.

Within days the majority of the non-Muslim population of West Punjab had "landed" in East Punjab which was a relatively small area and much poorer in resources. The new international border, known as the Radcliffe Line, had been drawn right down the middle of Lahore and Amritsar. On both sides, people scrambled to get onto the "right" side of the border. If they resisted, they, were violently forced out of their homes by their erstwhile neighbours. At least 10 million people fled north or south – depending upon their faith – in this great melee, and it is believed that about two million more were killed in the exodus.

Trains full of refugees were set on fire by militants from both sides of the border and all the fleeing passengers massacred. The grand Province of Punjab lost the prosperous Divisions of Multan, Lahore and Rawalpindi with their fertile fields, prosperous shopping malls and model towns to Pakistan. Indian Punjab was left with just two Divisions, Jalandhar and Ambala, and the five Sikh princely states of Patiala, Nabha, Faridkot, Jind and Kapurthala. These proved to be havens of peace for the fleeing refugees.

On August 14, 1947, the Islamic Republic of Pakistan was officially established. The following day, August 15, 1947, the partitioned Republic of India was born.

Chapter V:
Building a New Life in Patiala

The English proverb *"A drowning man catches at a straw"* *"doobte ko tinke ka sahara"* implies the desperate state of an unfortunate person who depends upon frail and ordinary things to save him/her self.

In this darkest hour of her life she saw a silver lining in the black clouds overhead - the Sikh State of Patiala where she had her younger sister Mohinder Kaur and her husband Sardar Shamsher Singh resided.

Patiala State was the largest and the most important Sikh State during the British rule in India. It was a blessing that Sardarni Harbans Kaur had her youngest sister, Sardarni Mohinder Kaur living in Patiala. So, thinking that pre-ordained, she left Ferozepur and arrived with her eight children in the distant and unknown City of Patiala, far away from Multan.

Maharaja of Patiala Sir Yadavindra Singh

The full title of the Maharaja was "Maharajadhiraj" Sir Yadavindra Singh Mahendra Bahadur, GCIE, GBE (Jan 17, 1913 - June 17, 1974)

Maharaja Yadavindra Singh, the ruler of the princely Sikh State of Patiala, had announced that all refugees arriving from Pakistan would be welcome in his State. This Sikh State was given special blessings by Guru Har Rai, the seventh Guru of the Sikhs, who had uttered the blessings from the Sikh Holy Scriptures saying in Gurmukhi: "tera ghar mera aseh" meaning "Your house is my abode."

The Maharaja Yadavindra Singh was much adored by his subjects and they showed their utmost respect to him by lowering their eyes and bowing their heads on seeing him approach. The Maharaja himself had a majestic posture and as a true nationalist he was greatly disturbed by the events taking place during the partition of India. He became fully cognisant of the colossal human suffering being inflicted upon innocent population on religious grounds.

To remove their sufferings, insecurity and hunger, he voluntarily approved the resettlement of these refugees from areas of Punjab that were being annexed to Pakistan as well from the Muslim autonomous State of Bahawalpur. His generosity brought tens of thousands of refugees flocking into Patiala on lorries and on special trains. To accommodate this influx of humanity, the Patiala state government immediately established two refugee camps in the proximity of the City of Patiala. These camps were on land adjacent to the Gurdwara Dukh Niwaran Sahib and at Tripuri, near the town of Rajpura, a distance of approximately 15 miles from Patiala. In a short period of time from August to October 1947, these camps turned into sprawling tent cities. The refugees, found survival very hard, especially the old and the very young, who with utmost difficulty had managed to come this far and were physically emaciated and weak due to physical exhaustion and hunger. Some died soon after arrival and there heartbreaking scenes were the result of the pathetic medical facilities for the refugees at these camps.

Unique symbols of the princely State of Patiala 1947

Patiala State Postage

Flag of Patiala State with its distinct Insignia

Royal Coat of Arms

Postage envelopes with photo of King George VI

Sikh Soldiers of Patiala State Forces defenders of Kashmir

The Punjabi language dialect spoken in Patiala was somewhat different from the dialect spoken in Lahore, the centre of the Punjabi culture. Sardarni Harbans Kaur had become fluent in the Pothohari Punjabi dialect after her marriage as her husband was from Rawalpindi. She later became conversant with the Saraiki, that was spoken in Multan, Khanewal, Dera Ghazi Khan, Rajanpur and Jampur districts where her husband had been posted while in the police service. With her sharp intellect and exposure to these different spoken Punjabi dialects, she soon became conversant with the dialect of Patiala Punjabi. As one is exposed to such variations in dialects, many spoken words of the different dialects can be amusing.

For example in:

English: *Pleased to meet you*

Lahore Punjabi Dialect: *Tuhanu mil ke bahut khushi hoyi*

Pothohari Dialect: *Tusan ki milay tay baoo khushi oyee*

Multani (Saraiki) Dialect: *Tuanu mil ke bahut khushi thi e*

Patiala Dialect: *Thonu mil ke bahli khushi hai*

At her sister's home in Patiala, Sardarni Harbans Kaur quickly learnt about the city culture and the local government establishment. With her typical courage and self-confidence, she went to meet the Chairman of Patiala State Charities Board, Sardar Pritam Singh Karorhia, who turned out to be a very kind fatherly figure. After listening to her story and having seen for himself how brave she was, caring single-handed for her young family after being torn away from her roots and relatives and having arrived at a remote and strange city.

It was also during this time that the Muslim habitants of Patiala were abandoning their homes for their migration to safer places in the newly created Islamic Republic of Pakistan. Their abandoned homes were known as "evacuee property" for which a new department called "Office of Custodian of Evacuee Property" was created. The number of such houses was far short of the number required to house the large influx of refugees that were arriving from the killing grounds of West Punjab on a daily basis. These people had left behind all their properties and worldly belongings in their ancestral homes in West Punjab.

Each and every family arriving in Patiala wanted some kind of shelter and basic necessities and this was proving to be a huge burden for the Government of Patiala State and its administration, but they bore the responsibility with stoic determination, generosity and traditional Sikh hospitality.

After a few days of acclimatising herself, Sardarni Harbans Kaur reflected on the huge challenges and responsibilities that lay ahead for a single mother with eight dependent children. With utmost courage she planned a course of action for her children's future. She established the following objectives to be pursued, not necessarily in any order:

- *A place that is called home*

- *Education for her eight children*

- *Financial survival through employment and supplemented with grants*

- *Encouragement, guidance, settlement and marriages of the children*

- *Social networking through Gurbani & Sangat*

- *Guidance and help for other destitute widows who were in similar or worse situations.*

Her immediate challenge was to find a place to live, to get all the children admitted to schools and arrange for an independent livelihood through government assistance, grants and employment. In addition, she had also taken a pledge to help other destitute widows who were arriving in droves from West Pakistan and needed consolation, guidance and moral support.

In the local administration in India, connections mattered more than merit. She personally knew no one in this new place to steer her towards some course of action. Endowed with unique and exceptional courage, she decided to meet Sardarni Manmohan Kaur, the wife of Sardar Gian Singh Rarewala, Chief Minister of State of Patiala and East Punjab States Union (PEPSU), the highest official in the State. The meeting went very well as she was welcomed sympathetically. After listening to the sacrifices of her husband, Sardar Nanak Singh, in the freedom movement of India, Mrs Rarewala remarked, "Your husband was a great martyr who sacrificed his life for our country. You are most welcome." she continued, "You are not an ordinary person. You seem to be from a highly educated and well-to-do family. Circumstances have reduced you to this position. The shine of a diamond can be seen even through the dust."

Sardarni Harbans Kaur was deeply moved, having evoked such a sympathetic and spontaneous response from the wife of the Chief Minister and could not thank her enough. She realised that they were true Sikhs who lived according the highest traditions of the Sikh Faith.

Thus encouraged by her meeting with Sardarni Manmohan Kaur, Sardarni Harbans Kaur filled an application for the allotment of any house evacuated by a Muslim family who had left for Pakistan. Furthermore, a recommendation on her behalf was also made by one of the class fellows of her husband, Sardar Mohan Singh, who happened to be the Managing Director of State Bank of Patiala. In his recommendation he wrote "This woman is the widow of a great patriot, Sardar Nanak Singh, who was as dear to me as my own brother."

So many refugees were clamouring for living accommodation since there were many more refugee families than the number of houses vacated by their former Muslim owners. After nearly two weeks of waiting, the Custodian of Muslim Evacuees Property, Patiala, allotted House No. 75, Mohalla Mir Kundla, Patiala to the family. It was not an easy task to get an evacuee's house so quickly but she had managed this with strong letters of recommendations and stories of her husband's bravery and martyrdom and the sad plight she had found herself in with such a young family. Due to the desperate situation in which Sardarni Harbans Kaur was seen with her small orphaned children, the department dealing with Care and Resettlement of Refugees, finally allotted the house to Sardarni Harbans Kaur.

The former owner of the house, had been a coat merchant, had vacated the house and moved to Karachi, now in Pakistan. The house was located in a blind and narrow street, barely 5 feet wide, a cul-de-sac between the fort, Qila Mubarak, and Saifabadi Gate.

One had to be careful entering and leaving the house as the other houses in this narrow street would discharge their daily discharge directly onto the street as there were no down spouts to contain the garbage in one spot.

For the boys it was fun to watch donkeys straddled with loads of bricks on either side from a nearby brick kiln entering the narrow street to deliver their load to residents on the street who needed bricks for repairs and renovations to their properties. These donkeys were not able to make a u-turn to exit and had to go all the way to end of this blind alley to turn around.

Donkeys loaded with bricks

The allotted house was a blessing even though it was in the rundown part of town but it served her and her young family well and provided somewhere she could nurture the children. It was a two story house, with one bedroom, a living room and a store room downstairs and one bedroom upstairs. There was also one small room at the mezzanine level. The house had no public sewage, no cooking gas. It had 240 volt electricity outlets but no telephone connection. Cold running tap water was available for about two hours each morning, afternoon and evening. With no large water storage containers with the family of eight children and one adult, shortage of water would have been quite problematic but for the fact that the previous owner had built up a ten-gallon concrete storage tank joined to the wall next to the water tap. This water tank was a great blessing in meeting the daily water needs of the large growing family.

To her good luck the corner grocery store was owned by a pious man, Lala Atma Ram, and this proved to be a blessing in the long run. With irregular and often insufficient income, the grocery and other essentials were made available on credit which helped her to keep the food on the table for her children. During these trying times Sardarni Harbans Kaur would also use her "Singer" sewing machine that had been wisely rescued from Multan with the forethought of mending and stitching old clothes for herself and her children. She had also managed to salvage some of her jewellery which she kept with trustworthy friends for safekeeping for a rainy day to meet unexpected family needs. Those were really very difficult and dark days for Sardarni Harbans Kaur but she never deviated from her focus of raising her family and helping the others in similar situations.

At this time she came upon a hidden steel safe embedded in one of the closets of the house they had moved into. Being in extreme poverty and with so many mouths to feed and overdue bills to be paid she struggled with her conscience to overcome the temptation to break into the safe to find some cash or jewellery left by the previous Muslim owner. She prayed to her inner soul, "O God reach out to me and prevent me from taking this booty." Using money that was not hers would not be morally right. Which mother knowingly can feed poison to her own children?

Some friends suggested that since she was in dire need and the owner had fled the land it was quite acceptable to open the safe and use the money and any valuables inside for her daily expenses and the children's education, to which she replied, "I can't do it. I trust God to feed my children. God has already given us shelter and bare necessities." She added, "This is like poison for me. I cannot take it. Whatever is in this safe belongs to its rightful owner or the public authorities." She then quoted from the Sikh Scriptures:

ਹਕੁ ਪਰਾਇਆ ਨਾਨਕਾ ਉਸੁ ਸੂਅਰ ਉਸ ਗਾਇ ॥

ਗੁਰੁ ਪੀਰ ਹਾਮਾ ਤਾ ਭਰੇ ਜਾ ਮੁਰਦਾਰੁ ਨ ਖਾਇ ॥

To take what rightfully belongs to another, is like a Muslim eating pork, or a Hindu eating beef. – (Guru Granth Sahib Ji page 141)

So she bravely went to the police station at Qila Mubarak and said, "There is a safe in my house. Please take it away."

The Inspector Prithi Pal Singh was amazed that despite her own poverty she had acted with such honesty and integrity showing a very high character. He praised her honesty by saying, "There was no way we would have known about a safe in your house. You are really a lady with a rich background even though right now you are a refugee from Pakistan".

After an hour or so, the police inspector arrived at the house with two constables. They had to struggle to detach the safe from its deep concrete foundation but they succeeded in the end, after using crow bars they moved the safe out of the house. While this was going on several people gathered in the street and watched the police struggling to move the safe away. Some were convinced that it held a lot of cash since it had belonged to a rich coat merchant. Everyone praised Sardarni Harbans Kaur's high character and her honesty, the Sikh way of thinking.

Nearly six months later when the communal frenzy had died down, to everyone's surprise the owner of the house returned from Karachi and came to the house. After introducing himself he enquired about the safe, saying that he had put the family treasures in the safe since it was dangerous to travel with valuables safely in those days. He was told politely that the safe had been handed over to pubic authorities. Since the safe was very heavy and embedded in a concrete foundation he could not even imagine that it had been removed and taken away by the local authorities. He turned around disappointed and left. He never came back.

Realising the need for proper nutrition for her eight growing children and experiencing the delivery of adulterated milk by the local milkman "gawala" at exorbitant prices, Sardarni Harbans Kaur decided to invest in a buffalo to provide milk and milk products for the young family. The elder sons would feed and milk the buffalo, taking turns to do so. It may seem strange now but keeping a buffalo at home was the normal practice for most residents of Patiala and perhaps for the rest of Punjab as well. After milking was done, Sardarni Harbans Kaur would churn the yogurt and say her prayers extempore at the same time. It was her firm belief that the butter produced with prayer on one's lips improved one's thinking and brought prosperity to those who eat it.

Churning yogurt for butter and butter milk

She was often asked "Why do you keep a buffalo with all the bother it entails?" To which she would reply, "Buffalo milk has many qualities. It is rich in energy and the fat in it is good for the growing children. They are all studying and will remain bright and smart at school." In the Sikh scriptures there is also a reference to the life of "Mata" Khivi who served milk products to Guru's congregation.

Mata Khivi (1506–1582) the wife of Guru Angad Dev, second Sikh Guru.

Since buffalos were kept in the courtyards of the houses, they needed grazing and exercise. For this, there were herdsmen who would go street to street and collect the buffalos from homes to join the herd. The herd of about 30-40 buffalos would then be chaperoned to the grazing areas outside the City limits for approximately four to six hours each day. On return from the grazing lands, these buffalos seemed to remember the streets and their own dwellings. Upon entering their own home yard, they would anxiously crave a healthy meal of wheat chaff mixed with soaked cotton seeds and mustard husk. They would also be fed with chopped corn stumps and would drink a bucket of water two to three times a day. The buffalo was milked twice a day, yielding an average of 15 litres of milk per day. Sardarni Harbans Kaur bought newly harvested wheat chaff during the harvest season in bulk to last her the full year. There was plenty of milk and milk products for her family.

As her mental state was now settled she began to focus her full attention on the schooling of her children. The eldest son, Rajinder, was fifteen years old and had missed his final Matriculation Examination for the Panjab University, Lahore, in March 1947 by a week because of the tragedy which had struck the family and forced them to flee. Rajinder had worked hard and was well prepared for the final examination.

Now that the family was safely settled in Patiala, Rajinder prayed to God that he be admitted to join Mahendra College in Patiala without having to show his Matriculation Certificate.

When the college reopened on 1st September 1947 after the summer holidays, Rajinder went to see the Principal Sardar Teja Singh, and requested that he be admitted to the two year Faculty of Arts programme of the Panjab University. In the meanwhile, the University in Lahore had relocated to a temporary facility in Solan in the Shimla Hills, which was a District of East Punjab. The Principal showed a great understanding because of the tragic political collapse of India and gave him permission to join classes at college immediately.

Mahendra College Patiala. Established 1875

Sardarni Harbans Kaur was delighted with Rajinder's admission to college without having to show the Matriculation certificate as a result of the exceptional circumstances surrounding his case. She could now see the prospect of her eldest son studying for a degree and then getting a well-paid job to support the family.

Rajinder was awarded The Panjab University Diploma of Faculty of Arts in 1949. By maintaining first position in several subjects and for his academic excellence at College, he was recognised at the annual Convocation by His Highness, the Maharaja of Patiala who personally awarded him seven books, one per subject in which he had been first in class.

After two years' diligence and dedicated hard work at college Rajinder moved on to the Third Year BA Course at the Panjab University. While studying at College, he by chance spotted a small notice in the newspaper about the Union Public Service Commission examination for admission into the Indian Military Academy at Dehra Dun to train as a cadet for a Commission in the Army. He took courage and applied and after a few days he was delighted to receive admission on merit to the prestigious Indian Military Academy at Dehra Dun where he started his training in January 1950. Here as a Gentleman Cadet, he was promoted to the prestigious rank of BCA (Battalion Cadet Adjutant). After two years of rigorous military training, he was granted a Permanent Regular Commission as a Second Lieutenant in the Indian Army in December 1951, an exceptional achievement for a boy who had become a refugee in his formative years.

During the period of upheaval from 1947-51, British officers from the Defence Forces of India as well as from central government Civil Service, Foreign Service, and others moved back to the United Kingdom leaving behind vacancies which were to be filled by Indians. Rajinder was well qualified to join any of these central government cadres, but his challenge was that these careers required money during the training period and since the Army training was free, he decided to go for the Army thereby becoming the trail blazer for four of his younger brothers who followed him into their own careers in the Indian armed forces. Needless to say, Sardarni Harbans Kaur was thrilled to see her eldest son in uniform as a military cadet and prayed to God to keep him safe in the wars and battles that lay ahead.

Photo taken on commissioning of eldest son Rajinder as Second Lieutenant in 1951
Sitting: Kulvinder, Brijinder, Raminder, Devinder
On chairs: Rajinder, mother Harbans Kaur, sister Surinder
Standing: Pritam, Rupinder

The next two sons, Pritam and Rupinder, were admitted to the BN Khalsa Polytechnic High School in Patiala and after completing their matriculation examinations in 1951, they also joined the Mahendra College for higher studies. The younger children attended grade schools and progressed academically. Pritam completed his B.A and B.Ed. and entered into the field of education. He served as a Head Teacher of the Agha Khan School in Mafia Island, near Dar-e-Salam, Kenya. Later in 1957 he took up the post of Deputy Headmaster at Bomdi-La, in North East Frontier Agency, in India, presently known as Arunachal State. Incidentally, he was part of the delegation that welcomed His Holiness the Dalai Lama who crossed over to India from Tibet in 1958. Rupinder followed in the footsteps of his oldest brother, Rajinder, and joined the Indian Military Academy at Dehra Dun, in January 1955 and was commissioned in the Corps of Engineers as Second Lieutenant in December 1956.

The younger boys also focused on their professional careers in the Indian Army and the Indian Air Force following in the footsteps of their elder brothers. Devinder and Kulvinder both joined the Indian Army as Second Lieutenants, while Brijinder joined the Indian Air Force as a Pilot Officer. The only daughter, Surinder, after completing her B.A. and B.Ed married an Army Officer, Saranjit Singh Sahney, who later retired in the rank of Brigadier. The youngest son, Rami, who was born posthumously in July 1947, completed his B.A from Panjab University and migrated to the United Kingdom in 1968. He has risen in business to be a millionaire as the result of sheer hard work, integrity and business acumen. His exemplary achievements in business have earned him five consecutive Queen's Awards for British Exports. He was honoured by the Queen as a Member of the British Empire (MBE) and later a CBE (the Commander of the British Empire) in 2016.

Each one of Sardarni Harbans Kaur's eight children excelled in their chosen fields. This in itself is an outstanding legacy for a woman who found herself widowed at such a young age and despite her own grief and personal loss, encouraged them at every step of way in their lives to excel in whatever they decided to do as honest citizens and proud Sikhs.

CHAPTER VI:
A Pillar of the Community

Having found a foothold in Patiala, the family settled in. The next worry for Sardarni Harbans Kaur was to secure some form of income through employment.

Undeterred by adversity, Sardarni Harbans Kaur, displayed her strong character and resolve and kept on trying for employment until she succeeded. She had knocked on every Government door for help in order to stand on her own feet and had approached public officials, government departments and welfare organisations for whatever help they could provide in that year of general disaster.

Finding a way out from the hundreds and thousands of those desperately struggling for survival was a Herculean task in itself and she fought for her survival and that of her children with the utmost resolve and ingenuity. She looked into herself and discovered the source of strength within that enabled her to face the challenges ahead. She vehemently believed that strength did not come from physical capacity but from an indomitable spirit.

For their immediate stop gap financial needs, leading Sikh organisations had come to the rescue, the Chief Khalsa Diwan, Amritsar, sanctioned the financial aid of Rs. 30 per month for five years. Later, the "Dharam Arth" (Religious Charity) Committee, a department under the kind hearted Sardar Pritam Singh Karorhia, sanctioned a grant of Rs. 30 per month for five years. The Chairman of the Punjab Riot Sufferers' Relief Committee, Chief Minister of Punjab, Bhim Sen Sachar, also provided a similar monthly monetary support. These amounts may look trivial today, but they had a reasonable buying power for basic necessities at that time. With this immediate financial support Sardarni Harbans Kaur learnt to manage her expenses very prudently. These monthly grants were a life saver but offered minimum rehabilitation as they were a recognition of her husband, Sardar Nanak Singh's inspiring political leadership during the pre-independence freedom movement and his ultimate sacrifice. However, they helped her to be recognised as a deserving person of significant importance. Under these trying conditions, she displayed her finest Sikh character and resolved to pull through the quagmire of problems.

To demonstrate her originality and outgoing character, she was one of the very few widows who dared to seek a personal audience with the top echelons of government, politicians and religious institutions. She was received by Sardar Baldev Singh, the first Defence Minister of independent India, Sardar Swaran Singh, India's Foreign Minister, Sardar Hukam Singh, Speaker of the Lok Sabha (Lower House of Indian Parliament), Bhim Sen Sachar, Chief Minister of Punjab, to name just a few. She also met Master Tara Singh, leader of the Sikhs, President of Shromani Gurdwara Parbandhak Committee, Chief Khalsa Diwan, and and many others. To meet these VVIPs, she travelled by buses and trains undertaking arduous journeys. Patiala railway station was on a branch line of the Indian Railways which caused more discomfort requiring her to change trains at Ambala Cantonment, the hub for other main line stations. There were no air conditioned luxury buses in those days and the roads were notoriously bumpy, full of potholes and in a state of disrepair.

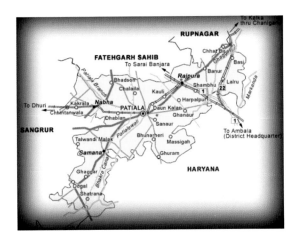

Patiala on branch line of Indian Railways

At that time Master Tara Singh, the charismatic and popular Sikh leader, came to Patiala and met Sardarni Harbans Kaur. Upon meeting her, he enquired after her health and about the education of her children. He felt distraught in seeing the plight of a well-to-do prominent Sikh family who had been uprooted from West Punjab. All he could do was to give her some money for her daily expenses and for her to buy books for the children, since he regarded the children as a precious heritage of the nation.

Master Tara Singh, affectionately known as "Masterji" took the written job application from Sardarni Harbans Kaur and gave it to Sardar Gian Singh Rarewala, the Chief Minister of PEPSU (Patiala and East Punjab States Union) and said, "This woman is from the house of Sardar Nanak Singh, Advocate, who was a great freedom fighter and was committed to keep India United ("Akhand Bharat") at all costs. He was a man of high character and exceptionally brilliant. He was an honorary worker of the Panth, Sikh faith."

To accommodate the large influx of refugees arriving every day, the Patiala state government had set up two refugee camps, one at Baba Jassa Singh Dera and the other at Tripuri near gurdwara Dukh Niiwaran Sahib, a historical Sikh shrine in the city. Unfortunately, the princely state of Bahawalpur was also now in Pakistan which resulted in Patiala receiving even more refugees. Recognising Sardarni Harbans Kaur as an outgoing and very capable person, the Chief Minister Sardar Gian Singh Rarewala, requested that she take up employment looking after the refugees in the camp which had been established at Tripuri. That was a blessing for her as it provided her with some stability in her life with a regular income providing security for her family.

Tents in a refugee camp

The Refugee camps were crowded and cramped and looked like a sea of tents forming an improvised housing colony. Due to a lack of proper sanitation there were outbreaks of typhoid and cholera and many refugees died due to malnutrition and a lack of proper medical care while sheltering in the tents. One day she saw two people whom she recognised as her own bedraggled and distraught parents. They had been part of a foot convoy from Gujranwala via Lahore and Amritsar. They were among the lucky few to have survived the frenzied and murderous Muslim gangs along the way. But sadly, the arduous journey had taken its toll and they did not survive for long due to fatigue, deprivation and malnutrition. Seeing her parents in this state and witnessing their untimely demise was heartbreaking for Sardarni Harbans Kaur.

She was also distressed when she recognised the family of her husband's younger sister Partap Kaur, affectionately known as "Kauran". She was there with her husband Sangat Singh and their two sons and three daughters. Her teenage son, Pritpal, who was full of bubbling enthusiasm for life despite all the adversities he faced, contracted typhoid and died. His parents were grief stricken and shattered having lost the darling of their family. His untimely death was mourned by everyone in the camp. It is very difficult to describe the scenes of misery, grief and poverty that the once affluent people of Punjab were undergoing. It can be said that this period of their lives was easily the darkest.

As an additional act of dedication, Sardarni Harbans Kaur voluntarily started to gather all the small children for their initial lessons in Panjabi and basic arithmetic as many children had not attended a school for several months. Teaching these small children at the camp not only benefitted the children by keeping them out of mischief but also kept Sardarni Harbans Kaur occupied. She needed this diversion as the camp was full of grieving widows and orphaned children who were suffering and she too was grieving herself but carried the unbearable pain in her heart silently.

After nearly two years, these camps started to wind down. At about this time one young woman from the princely State of Bahawalpur approached Sardarni Harbans Kaur and stated that she lived in a house full of other refugees but had no means of support and could not afford to feed herself. After listening to her sorrowful story Sardarni Harbans Kaur asked her to work in her own house to cook food for her family and look after them while she was out at work. She gladly accepted her offer and this wonderful lady worked at her house for the next 13 years. She cooked appetising food and the children used to fight for her delicious chapaties that were round and perfectly risen. The children called her "Ama Ji" as mark of respect. "Ama Ji," is a name that is used to address one's own mother.

One day after her morning prayers Sardarni Harbans Kaur was witness to a miracle. She saw a falcon circling overhead and then eventually settle down on top of the dome of Gurdwara Dukh Niwaran Sahib. She also saw many devotees looking up to the sky and gathering hurriedly around the Gurdwara. Everyone believed that Guru Gobind Singh had sent his falcon to assure them of His powerful and protective presence.

Guru Gobind Singh, 10th living Guru of the Sikhs with his falcon (hawk)

The falcon made Sardarni Harbans Kaur even more determined in her resolve to succeed against all odds. She was inspired by the sight and took it as a message from heaven. This realisation struck her suddenly and she said to the amazement of the onlookers. "We are proud Sikhs of Guru Gobind Singh. The word 'refugee' does not exist in our vocabulary. And we will rise against all odds."

She emphasised to her own children the need to study hard in order to qualify so that they could get good jobs to earn their living with honesty and dignity. She also taught them that it was important to inspire and help others not as fortunate as them. After that day her children never looked back, or felt sorry for themselves. She was glad to see that with her guidance all her children were inspired and brought honour to their "Shaheed" father's name.

On the last day at the refugee camp everyone joined in praying together in Gurdwara for the last time before dispersing and going their different ways. Sardarni Harbans Kaur was asked to address the congregation and say a few words. She felt greatly honoured since she had been working with devotion as a humble servant of her divine Gurus. After some hesitation she stood up to speak. The keynote of her speech was that the teachings of Guru Nanak Dev should be followed and the spirit of the Tenth Guru, Guru Gobind Singh acquired. In her address to the fellow sisters in grief there was one sentence that was her own belief. "The word 'refugee' does not exist in the Sikh vocabulary." That is exactly what she used to say to her own children. She encouraged them to do their best to succeed in life under the motto, "Charhdi Kala" (high spirits) and "Guru Raakha,"(God will protect you.).

During the time at the refugee camp, Sardarni Harbans Kaur witnessed some very corrupt and immoral practices from the contractor who used to bring the rations of whole wheat flour, grain, vegetables and lentils for the inhabitants. She saw that he was a very dishonest man and that he used to mix barley with the wheat. She confronted him, saying "The wheat flour you are delivering to the Camp is adulterated. It is mixed with barley flour. You should not do this to the poor refugees who have already lost everything." He denied doing anything wrong and this left her speechless.

The next day she walked to the flour mill and saw him bring wheat to be ground into flour. It was a large quantity and the grinding took nearly all day. When it had been ground, he spread it on a large tarpaulin. He then started mixing ground barley flour with the wheat flour. She made herself known and asked: "Brother what are you doing? Why are you doing this?" He got very angry and told her to keep quiet and go away. She returned much saddened. That evening she prayed, "O God, protect us from these corrupt suppliers." But there was ultimate justice in God's dispensation. After some months Sardarni Harbans Kaur met him in Anardana Chowk, in down town Patiala. He looked depressed and miserable. She questioned him and he told her that his children had turned to a life of crime. He said, "My children have turned to crime." She noticed that his hands were covered in festering sores and said, "Evil deeds bring retribution."

Another time, she found that the man delivering milk was equally corrupt. He used to add water to the milk that he delivered to the camp. Sardarni Harbans Kaur wanted to confirm her suspicion so one day at the crack of dawn she, along with an assistant, went to his dairy farm. The farm consisted of aged mud walls around the buffalo shed where the buffalos were milked. Through a crack in the wall she was able to see everything on the other side. She saw the man, take a half filled bucket of milk to the tap and and mixed it up with water. Courageously she went in. "What are you doing, brother?" He was startled and he replied, "Don't interfere in my work. Go away." Once again she returned home much saddened and came down with an attack of pneumonia due to her exposure to the cold so early in the morning. But God listened to her prayers and she recovered within a few weeks.

Finally the refugee camps closed down after about three months which left Sardarni Harbans Kaur jobless once again. By this time her reputation as a compassionate person was well established in the community. The office of Custodian for Muslim Evacuee Properties had created a vacancy for a Rent Collector. The authorities approached Sardarni Harbans Kaur if she would be interested in this position. This offer came as a God sent opportunity to her and she gladly accepted it.

Upon joining, she immediately familiarised herself with her duties and responsibilities. These evacuee properties were rented out mostly to the widows. There were invariably more applicants than the available properties and the situation was desperate.

The evacuees' houses were allotted on a first come first served basis. However, in reality the person in charge used to allot the houses in a numbered order but by leaving a few blank spaces in-between before entering the names of the applicants. It was a common practice to accept bribes and enter the later applicant's name on a blank line. Her boss suggested that she should follow this practice and share the bribe money. She declined to be involved in this sinful activity. Her boss angrily said to her "Since you have started working here, my 'under the table' extra income has decreased drastically."

One day a woman came into the office and offered Sardarni Harbans Kaur her gold ring as a bribe to obtain an evacuee's house saying, "I have been staying with a relative who has small children and she cannot house me anymore. I must find somewhere else to live. I am in a terrible situation." When questioned about her husband, the woman replied "I am from Rawalpindi where a genocide took place. My husband was killed in the most brutal manner, leaving me and my little children fatherless with nowhere to live. Please take my gold ring. It is my last possession."

Sardarni Harbans Kaur embraced her and said, "Keep it and use it for your children's education. I cannot take it. I cannot give 'poison' to my own children to eat, nor will this ring go with me to the next world after my death." The distraught woman replied "You are a true follower of Guru Nanak. I wish to touch your feet". Sardarni Harbans Kaur immediately asked her to take those words back and emphasised that she was the humblest servant in the House of Guru Nanak.

She recalled the story of Bhagat Kabir ji. One morning before dawn goddess Lakshmi appeared in his dream. She said, "Sing God's praises and I will enrich you with double your wealth." Bhagat Kabir said, "Excessive wealth and possessions (Maya) are like the snake that bites the one that feeds it."

Once the situation was under control, The Department of Custodian of Muslim Evacuee Properties started to wind down as well. Then what next for Sardarni Harbans Kaur? She reflected on her life before Partition and how she had organised adult literacy classes for women and girls on a voluntary basis during 1943-44, when she had taught them Punjabi language at her residence as well as at the local Gurdwara in Rajanpur, Jampur and Dera Ghazi Khan. She had been ahead of her contemporaries then and she remained a role model for the women in that remote part of Punjab that lay beyond the River Indus.

With her usual resourcefulness and community contacts, Sardarni Harbans Kaur managed to secure a temporary teaching job at the Government Primary School, Sheranwala Gate Patiala. Recognising that her handicap was a lack of formal teaching credentials, she immediately thought of furthering her own education at the minimum level to qualify for a permanent teaching post. To achieve this goal, she enrolled for a diploma programme of Proficiency in Panjabi (Buddhiman-Modern Indian Languages) at Panjab University. Despite the heavy work load, caring for her children and looking after the house at the same time, she was determined to succeed. After an intensive study, she passed the final examination and was awarded the Diploma in Modern Indian Languages in August 1952. She had accomplished this by studying late at night after her working hours and she was determined to gain knowledge from whichever source it came. In her philosophical thoughts she felt that in reality a human being was continuously learning throughout life. Each person has something to contribute to the common good.

Recognising her new academic credentials, her teaching position became permanent at the same Government Primary School. Whilst in service, she also completed the Teachers' Special Certificate from the Department of Education, PEPSU in 1956. She completed her teaching assignment with devotion and dedication for which she was recognised by the Government of Punjab and was awarded the State Award for being teacher of outstanding merit in the State in 1968. The Governor of Punjab personally presented her with the State Award at a Convention "in recognition of her valuable services to the community as a teacher of outstanding merit." The Award was signed by Sardar Trilochan Singh, the

Education Commissioner and Secretary to the Government of Punjab, and Mr PL Sondhi, Director of Public Instruction, Punjab.

By this time her three elder sons, Rajinder, Pritam and Rupinder, had entered the work force - in 1951, 1955 and 1956 respectively. They still carried with them the deep feelings of grief having seen their father brutally assassinated by Islamic terrorists on March 5, 1947 and they relived the sight of him lying in the morgue with a bandaged head and several stab wounds to his body. Despite their very young age they all decided instinctively to stand by their mother and give her the utmost support for the survival of the family, making sure that under the guidance of their charismatic mother, the younger siblings too attained their full potential in life.

Pritam moved to Kenya and the army life took Rajinder and Rupinder to far off operational areas separated by thousands of miles. All three sons would make extreme sacrifices to save the maximum from their monthly income to send money back to their mother to supplement her income. This financial support ensured the continuity of education of her younger children. This resolve was subsequently carried out by all of her sons even after they were married and had their own families to look after. This dedicated financial support was a big sacrifice and continued for well over fifteen years by which time the family situation had greatly stabilised. It was due to the strong spiritual heritage as Sikhs and the deep love, hard work and loyalty shown by their mother that all her children stuck together to make so many sacrifices to support their mother for so many years.

Additionally, the government of Punjab had initiated a War Jagir Award (Grant) under the East Punjab Awards Act XXII of 1948 as amended to date. Eligible residents of Punjab were invited to apply for this War Jagir by parents who had sons serving in the Indian Armed Forces during the emergencies declared by the President of India under Article 352 of the

Constitution of India on October 26, 1962 and December 3, 1971. By this time Sardarni Harbans Kaur had five of her sons in the Armed Forces of the Union that qualified her for this War Jagir.

During the 1965 Indo-Pakistan war, all five of her sons were already commissioned officers and were deployed at the frontline in service of their motherland. When she applied for the War Jagir in 1966, her sons in the defence services were:

IC-5837 Major Rajinder Singh

IC-8135 Major Rupinder Singh

IC-14880 Capt Devinder Singh

IC-15491 Capt Kulvinder Singh and

9630 Pilot Officer Brijinder Singh, Indian Air Force

This information was certified by the Army Headquarters on March 29, 1966 and the War Jagir was sanctioned to Sardarni Harbans Kaur at the value of Rs. 180 per year for life.

Arranged marriages have been a part of the Indian culture. It is the responsibility of the parents to provide for the education and the marriage of their children. The parents' duties are not considered complete unless their children are married through the established system. This was an additional responsibility for Sardarni Harbans Kaur as her sons and daughter were now almost of marriageable age.

Luckily for her, because of her outgoing personality and by maintaining social contacts with the community and her ever helping attitude, she became well known in the Sikh and Hindu communities at large. She would console others and happily share her family life with her friends and acquaintances. She expanded her social circle extensively with her active participation in social, religious and cultural events and because of this she would hear about well settled families from people in contact with her.

Over time, she had developed a vast contact list within the community. When the time was ripe to arrange the marriages of her children, she was able to choose brides from well-educated and progressive families. Due to her efforts, all of her eight children were well settled in married life and she was blessed with good daughters-in-law and many wonderful grandchildren.

Awards and Certificates

Panjab University Modern Indian Languages

Proficiency in Panjabi (Budhiman) (1952)

Patiala and East Punjab States Union Education Department

Teacher's Special Certificate (1956)

GOVERNMENT OF PUNJAB

Education Department

This State Award is given to ਸ਼੍ਰੀਮਤੀ ਹਰਬੰਸ ਕੌਰ, ਵੀਰ, of ਗੌ. ਪ੍ਰਾਇਮਰੀ ਸਕੂਲ, ਸ਼ੇਰਾਂਵਾਲਾ ਗੇਟ, ਪਟਿਆਲਾ in public recognition of his/her valuable services to the community as a teacher of outstanding merit.

Director of Public Instruction,
PUNJAB.
Chandigarh
DATED: 5-9-1968

Education Commissioner
AND
Secretary to Government Punjab,
EDUCATION DEPARTMENT.

Education Department: State Award for valuable services to the community as a teacher of outstanding merit (1959)

Sanad of War Jagir
Granted for Meritorious Service rendered during the Emergency 1965
Government of Punjab

News published in the provincial daily

PUNJAB GOVERNMENT WILL HONOUR 12 TEACHERS

From Our Special Correspondent

CHANDIGARH Aug 29, 1966 - The Punjab Government has decided to honour six primary and six secondary school teachers selected from all over the State for their meritorious services to the teaching profession.

At a function to be held at Patiala on the Teachers' Day, September 5, Governor D.C. Pavate, will give each of them a cash reward of Rs 500 and a commendation certificate.

The six secondary school teachers selected for the award are: Mr. Boota Singh, Principal G.N. Khalsa High School, Batala, Smt. Bhagwanti Bawa, Principal, Government Girls High School, Amritsar, Mr. Kans Raj, Headmaster, Government High School, Jungal (Gurdaspur district), Mr. Joginder Singh, Headmaster, Khalsa High School, Sohana, Mr. Samand Singh, Headmaster, B.Z.F. Khalsa High School, Sirhind, and Mr. Amrit Lal, Master, Government Sports School, Jullundur.

*The primary school teachers are Mr. Gopal Krishan, Mr.Darbara Singh, Mr. Tej Pal, Mr. Rattan Lal Bhatnagar, Mr. Joginder Singh and **Smt. Harbans Kaur.***

Recipients of the State Awards with Dr. D. C. Pavate, Governor, Punjab, who presented these awards on Teachers' Day at the State College of Education, Patiala, on Thursday. The Vice-Chancellor, Mr. Kirpal Singh Narang, is standing near the Governor.

Harbans Kaur is standing in the front row with meritorious certificate in her hands.

CHAPTER VII:
Moving from Patiala to Chandigarh to London

Sardarni Harbans Kaur was a woman of great vision and far sightedness. She was strong and courageous and had full faith in the Sikh scriptures that would guide her destiny to her desired destination. She carefully listened to her inner self with strength and courage which had showed her the ability to overcome the adversities befallen her. She gave her children the best chance and opportunity in life through her personal sacrifices as well as constant encouragement by continuously reminding her children of "CHARHDI KALA" and "RABB RAKHA". (High spirits and May God protect you!)

By this time five of her sons were serving in the defence forces and were posted to far flung active duty, non-family field locations or were at peace stations in places hundreds of miles away. Her daughter was married and had moved out and her youngest son, Rami, had moved to London in 1968. This growth of the family progressively shrank the size of the family at home as the children, after completing their training, were posted all across India, several hundreds of miles away from Patiala. Having been used to the bustle of a large family, she suddenly found herself alone in Patiala, as an empty nester.

She started to feel lonely and needed some close relatives nearby. As luck would have it, her younger brother Sardar Faujdar Singh and his wife Sardarni Harbhajan Kaur had settled in Chandigarh, which was approximately 30 miles away from Patiala. The capital of undivided Punjab, Lahore, had been awarded to Pakistan in 1947 by the Radcliffe Boundary Commission responsible for demarcating areas to be carved out for Pakistan. The modern City of Chandigarh became the new capital of Punjab State. Its architecture and urban planning was done by Swiss architect, Le Carbusier, and the new City was built during the 1950s.

Sardar Faujdar Singh suggested to his sister to move to Chandigarh to live close to their residence. Welcoming his suggestion, she put her house at 75 Mir Kundla, Patiala on sale and it was sold within 3-4 months. With her brother's efforts a house was found for her across the road from his own house in Chandigarh. She felt a great sense of relief when she moved into her new home in 1966. Her brother's family would take good care of her. Whenever special meals were prepared in their house, she would be invited to join them and if it was late in the evening, her nephew, Daljit Singh, would come over to her house with warm and freshly cooked meals. Her brother and his family looked after her with great care and affection.

At that time, a new Gurdwara in Sector 15-C was under construction. Sardarni Harbans Kaur took an active interest in this project, organising and performing "Kar Sewa" for timely completion of this project. The Gurdwara was named Gurdwara Sri Guru Arjan Dev Ji, in memory of the fifth guru of the Sikhs.

Guru Arjan Dev
(15 April 1563 – 30 May 1606)

Guru Arjan Dev was responsible for compiling the gurbani writings for the Sikh Holy Book, Guru Granth Sahib.

She participated in religious activities and became a regular devotee at the Gurdwara in Chandigarh. She would perform kirtan, deliver religious discourses and addressed the congregation on Sikh historic events on religious themes. Thereby, she established a healthy lifestyle as a useful member of the community.

Once she felt settled at Chandigarh, Sardarni Harbans Kaur turned to voluntary service within the community. She donated a harmonium to the Government Primary School in Sector 24 in Chandigarh for the children to use in their music classes. Both the children and staff were delighted to receive this gift. The Principal would often invite her to come to the School to teach "shabads" and "bhajans" to the children. This was a joyful service for her, to introduce spiritual music to children and she found real joy in directing them towards the divine path. This particular School had a lot of "Harijan" (impoverished) students, these distressed children could not afford writing materials, so often, Sardarni Harbans Kaur would write down "bhajans" and "shabads" on paper to give to them. They were eager to learn them by heart and started reading Gurbani and Bhajans at home too. Thus family values were strengthened in their homes. But things were not to stay this way for long.

By 1968, her sons Rajinder, Pritam and Rami and their families were settled in London, England. They beseeched her to move to London to be a part of her larger family of children and grand children. As her remaining sons were still serving in the defence services they were transferred every two years or so to other non-family operational areas or to peace stations in different geographical regions of India with different cultures and where they spoke different regional languages. This unique family situation meant that she was alone in Chandigarh away from her nuclear family. She was also growing older.

She was happy with the suggestion of her sons living abroad and moved to London in 1977. Initially, she lived there with her second elder son, Pritam Singh and his wife Parminder Kaur (Noni), enjoying the bliss of living with her own family. During her stay with them she actively participated in the social life of the local community. A few months later, her youngest son, Rami and his wife Renu, requested that she moved to live with them to be among their small children. Sardarni Harbans Kaur moved to their home and stayed with them enjoying her life with her three youngest grand children. She lived with them for more than a decade. The grand children grew up and started attending school and the house felt empty once again as Rami and Renu also went to work.

When her daughter Surinder Kaur Sahney and son-in-law Brigadier Saranjit Singh Sahney visited London on a short trip from India, Sardarni Harbans Kaur expressed her desire to live nearer to a Gurdwara where she could spend some time in meditation and in the company of "sangat" (religious congregation). This was her sincere and emotional desire. Her daughter was already aware that Southall, a district of London, had a sizeable population of Indian and Pakistani residents that would provide a social and cultural atmosphere for her mother. With her outstanding efforts, an assisted housing Council flat at 6, Belmont Avenue, Southall, was allotted to her and she moved there in 1988. This house was in close proximity of Sri Guru Singh Sabha Gurdwara on Havlock Road, Southall.

The sizeable Asian community in Southall provided a feeling of being "back home" to Sardarni Harbans Kaur with many Indian and Pakistani residents hailing from rural areas of East and West Punjab. They were often lacking communication skills within the English speaking country and their social contacts were limited to within their own surrounding communities. The arrival of Sardarni Harbans Kaur amidst them was a great event, particularly for the women folk who shared their domestic issues frankly and in confidence with her. They also sought guidance from her on family and social matters freely speaking in their mother tongue, the Punjabi or the Urdu languages. For many she was the source of knowledge and for others she was a source of inspiration.

Sardarni Harbans Kaur soon became well entrenched in this community and was greatly respected by these families as if she was their own mother. Whenever these families prepared any special meals, they would bring a portion of it for their "mother" as well. She was invariably invited to join Sikh, Hindu and Muslim religious celebrations, marriages and birthdays. Sometimes they brought their small children after school to learn Punjabi. Sardarni Harbans Kaur taught them with love and devotion and also told them stories of folklore from Punjab. On Sundays, she attended the Gurdwara, participated in langar sewa and sang Hymns (Kirtan) in praise of God. Many a time, she would give talks on the teachings of the Sikh Gurus and other contemporary issues relevant to the community. She lived there for 10 years and in this time she won the respect and admiration of all the families living in the local communities.

When her daughter Surinder Kaur Sahney, visited her again in 1993, she observed that her mother was very happy in her surroundings, and with her neighbours and the many, Hindus, Sikhs and Muslims and some from Afghanistan who resided there. Many Afghans had come to the UK seeking political asylum and these people from different areas and different backgrounds had developed a love and affection for Sardarni Harbans Kaur and treated her as they would treat their own mothers. Her next door neighbour, Nachhitar Singh, had requested that his wife and children serve hot food to her. Then there were Razia and Shaina and one Mr. Bhat from Pakistan who came from her own native city of Gujranwala. Surinder, was thrilled to see her mother amidst a much larger family, where someone would come and iron her clothes, or come to her to seek guidance for their domestic problems.

The word of her outreach gradually became known across Great Britain. Many officials would call on her to listen to her passion for helping the needy, especially the women, from the larger communities of South East Asia. Many admired her volunteer services in the Asian community. A renowned scholar from the California State University of San Francisco, California, Dr. Inderpal Grewal, Professor of English Language, visited her in England in 1987 to hear her ideas and recorded her contribution towards women's causes.

Thus Sardarni Harbans Kaur was recognised as a special woman in Southall who was active in the social and cultural issues concerning women in the area. For this she was recognised and received a prominent mention in the book *Women of Substance, Profiles of Asian Women in the United Kingdom*, by Dr. Pushpinder Chowdhry. The researcher had identified around 200 women in Great Britain from the Asian population who were making their mark in the diverse fields within the society. These identified women are incontestable role models who have demonstrated courage and determination to lead their way in enriching the Asian Community.

Women of Substance

Women of Substance, Profiles of Asian Women in the UK
by Pushpinder Chowdhry
(Hansib Publications.1997 ISBN: 1-870518-56-X). Page 74

Extract from *Women of Substance*

Harbans Kaur was born in Gujranwala, now Pakistan, on 15th March 1913. Afterwards she married Sardar Nanak Singh, a Prosecuting Inspector with the police on 7th August 1930. They had eight children - seven sons and one daughter.

Harbans' husband, a local leader and the president of Shromani Gurdwara Prabhandak Committee, (SGPC) opposed the partition of India on religious grounds. On 5th March 1947, students of DAV College in Multan, demonstrated against the imminent partition. Nanak Singh, being a local leader, went to the rescue of the students and was killed in the ensuing riots. He was honoured by the community and his picture now hangs in the Shaheeed gallery in the Golden Temple in Amritsar, along with other martyrs.

Widowed at the age of 34, Harbans Kaur, along with her eight children was forced to leave her native land and settled in Patiala, India. She refused to give up her children to an to an orphanage, and decided to cope with the tremendous responsibility of bringing them up alone. Joining the Punjab Government as a rehabilitation officer, she helped to settle the refugees who were victims of partition. She encouraged and supported her children to study hard. Five of her sons joined the defence services in India as commission officers. Two of her sons immigrated to the United Kingdom and now own successful businesses.

Harbans Kaur became a head teacher after completing her job as rehabilitation officer. Her five commissioned officer sons actively served for the defence services of India, as a result of this she was honoured by the Punjab Government a "Proudest Punjabi Mother." She received a war pension for their services to the Indian armed forces.

Harbans Kaur is an epitome of Indian women, instilling the same values to her daughter. In fact against all the odds, she rises above to do the best for her family and her country, India. She lived in Middlesex for many years, where she relaxed in the company of her two sons and her grand children.

On the front cover of their premier edition of *Being One* published in March 2003, the publishers recognising her as the most illustrious Sikh woman, prominently displayed her photo in the centre surrounded by several other women who were also recognised. She always remained a role model for women under the motto "Chardi Kala" meaning "High Spirits" and "High Morale". It is noteworthy that in this collage the author placed Sardarni Harbans Kaur's photo prominently in the middle among other achievers bringing out her established stature in the community as a role model for women to emulate.

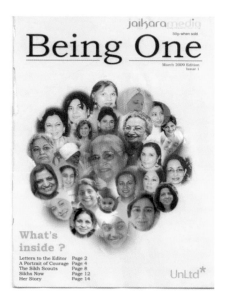

Being One **Published by Jaikaramedia**

For Sardarni Harbans Kaur her life was well fulfilled, organised and enjoyable. However in early December 1998 she slipped and fell in her home. This fall caused a hairline bone fracture and some minor pain. She did not realise that she had fractured a bone and thought that the discomfort would go away. The situation soon became aggravated as the fracture had resulted in internal bleeding. This caused the area to become septic and she had to be hospitalised for urgent medical attention.

Unfortunately, she did not recover from this injury and succumbed to her illness on January 25, 1999 at the age of 86. The funeral took place at the crematorium in Ruislip, West London, and prayers were said and tributes were paid at the Park Avenue Gurdwara in Southall. The High Commissioner of India in London sent his condolences to the bereaved family. Her ashes were immersed in River Thames by all of her sons and daughter.

OBITUARY - JANUARY 25, 1999

After retirement from service at Patiala Sardarni Harbans Kaur came to England to be with her youngest son who was doing very well in business. After nearly a decade, she moved to her own house in Southall where the last years of her life were devoted to service of community that included doing langar sewa at gurdwara, baby sitting for young working mothers, counseling young brides who were new to the West and were going through domestic strains and family tensions.

For those who left their own parents back in Punjab Sardarni Harbans Kaur was the mother. Very often these families showed their gratitude by bringing food and small presents.

For some she was the source of knowledge. For the others she was the source of inspiration. Those who saw her doing langar sewa and kirtan at gurdwara, and giving talks on Gurus' lives, regarded her as one of the most distinguished Sikh women of 20th century.

With her demise in Southall, England, on 25 January 1999, a heroic chapter in the aftermath of the partition of India in 1947, that played havoc with millions of lives, came to an end. She saw the destruction of West Punjab and the loss of Lahore, Gujranwala and Sri Nankana Sahib and countless Sikh institutions. After her own children had grown up, she devoted the rest of her life to the well-being of the community.

Now that Sardarni Harbans Kaur is no more in this world, we ought to celebrate her courage and sacrifices as well as the courage and sacrifices of countless other Sikh women throughout history by designating one day in the year to remind us of their good deeds and exemplary lives. This will serve as a source of inspiration to our future generations and keep the families united and strong.

It would be most appropriate to designate January 25th every year as the Sikh Women's Day, a day dedicated to reminding us all of the courage, sacrifices and "sewa" of Sardarni Harbans Kaur and of the glory of Sikh women throughout history.

CHAPTER VIII:
The Legacy of Sardarni Harbans Kaur, Her Sons & Daughter

Sardarni Harbans Kaur

These once poor, uprooted refugee and fatherless children guided by their widowed mother is a legacy left by their mother. She reinforced in her children the concept of inner strength and faith in Sikh gurbani for their success in life. The children too realised that through adversity they will seek the opportunity to grow and rise to their potentials.

The achievement of Sardarni Harbans Kaur is manifest in the outstanding achievements of each of her eight children under the unimaginable adverse and tragic circumstances of the 1947 partition of India. Her husband, Sardar Nanak Singh, who was assassinated in 1947 during the political turmoil in India is chronicled in the companion volume: *Don't Break up India*, published by Hemkunt Press, New Delhi, India, in 2005. The success story of each of her eight children is a living tribute to the legacy of the brave and proud Mother of India.

COLONEL RAJINDER SINGH, PSC, ARMY SERVICE CORPS & INTELLIGENCE BRANCH

**Defence Services
Staff College**

**Army Service Corps
and Intelligence
Branch**

Being the eldest son of Sardarni Harbans Kaur, he remembers being distraught whilst accompanying his mother with tears flowing down her cheeks to meet various senior officials of State.

"My mother narrated our tragedy of losing the bread winner in Multan and then fleeing as destitute in a penniless state. I must say that those high ups were very kind to my mother and listened to her sad tale with patience and did whatever they could to help our family. That included job for our mother, allotment of an evacuee's house and monetary allowance of Rs. 30 per month. With an additional sum of Rs. 30 per month coming to us from Chief Khalsa Diwan and some grant from the Punjab Riot Sufferers Relief Committee under Chief Minister Bhim Sen Sachar, our family survived on utmost basic necessities."

The breakthrough came unexpectedly when Rajinder saw a notice in a newspaper in the College library, inviting applications for Indian Military Academy as cadets in 1949. He took courage and without informing his mother, applied. He successfully passed the Union Pubic Services competitive written examination and thereafter within weeks he was invited to Services Selection Board at Meerut, Uttar Pradesh, and was selected to join the Army. He became Gentleman Cadet at the Indian Military Academy, Dehra Dun on 1st January 1950. During his two years of rigorous training, he was promoted as Battalion Cadet Adjutant and finally passed out high in the overall order of merit as Second Lieutenant on 30 December 1951. His commission was of immense benefit to the family as he started supporting mother wholeheartedly to the best of his ability.

The adversity in his childhood had taught him to beat the odds and excel in every field. While serving in the army he had the opportunity to do a two year course for Interpretership in the Persian language at the School of Foreign Languages, Government of India, New Delhi. At the same time he started studying the German language privately and passed both the examinations with Distinction. Later when the King of Afghanistan, Mohammed Zahir Shah and the President of Federal Republic of Germany, Heinrich Lübke visited India he was the official interpreter to both, a unique distinction for him.

In 1958 the Government of India appointed him as the official interpreter to His Majesty King Mohammed Zahir Shah of Afghanistan who was on official visit. He toured with the king to several institutions across India. The King was highly impressed by his command of Persian language and before his departure from India he presented him with an automatic gold watch bearing the Royal monogram of the King.

Royal emblem on the back of Gold watch made by IWC, Shaffhausen, Switzerland

His Majesty King Mohammed Zahir Shah of Afghanistan

Later, during the official visit of His Excellency Dr.Karl Heinrich Lübke, President of the Federal Republic of Germany, the Government of India appointed Rajinder as the official interpreter to the President. He maintained high level of linguistic fluency with proper pronunciation and intonation just like the native speakers of the German language. The President on leaving for Germany presented the book *Schoepfungen der indischer Kunst* as a token of his appreciation.

Heinrich Lübke, President of the Federal Republic of Germany 1959 to 1969

His Excellency President of the Federal Republic of Germany

Book - *Schoepfungen indischer Kunst*

PRITAM SINGH (1933 - 2005)

After completing his B.A. and B.Ed. from Panjab University, Pritam, took up a teaching assignment in a government Primary School in Chandigarh, the shared capital of Punjab and Haryana States. As a pioneer educationist, he discovered a challenging teaching position as Head Teacher in Bomdi-La, capital of West Kameng Division of North East Frontier Agency (NEFA) in 1957. NEFA was renamed as Arunachal Pradesh in 1972. In those days NEFA was a restricted area and one had to get a permit from the Government of India to enter any Sub Division of NEFA. Each Sub Division was administered by an appointed Political Officer.

Bomdi-La was accessible from the Foothill in Assam only by 4x4 jeeps over unpaved roads. But this did not deter Pritam and he accepted the job offer. He served at Bomdi-La from 1957 till 1963.

Sub Divisions of Arunachal Pradesh (formerly North East Frontier Agency)

NEFA is a tribal area and the inhabitants are influenced by the teachings of Lord Buddha.

Lord Buddha in Tawang Monastry

Typical Tribal Costume in NEFA

The Dalai Lama - Spiritual Leader of the Tibetans -
Nobel Peace Prize in 1989.

The uprising in Tibet against the Chinese invaders in 1959 forced the Dalai Lama to cross over to India in March 1959 to seek political asylum. He entered India at Twang in Western Kameng Frontier Division of NEFA, which the first entry point into India and Pritam was one of the few officials of the Indian delegation who welcomed the Dalai Lama to India at Twang.

Being adventurous, Pritam secured the teaching position in Mafia Island, off the coast of Dar-e-Salaam in Tanzania, in East Africa. Flying off from Dar-e-Salaam in 1964, he joined the Agha Khan High School in Mafia Island as Deputy Headmaster where he served from 1964 till 1967. He soon became very popular in this remote island. With his outgoing personality and strong communication skills, the local daily newspaper published from Dar-e-Salaam appointed him as their staff reporter for news from the island.

Mafia Island off the coast of Dar-e-Salaam, Tanzania (East Africa)

Now, he wanted to advance his professional credentials in education. He succeeded in securing a teaching post with the Inner London Department of Education in London, England. The farewell note published in the local daily expresses his contribution and attachment to the community. Sunday News, January 30, 1965.

The Mafia Island newspaper clipping above reads as below:

The people of Mafia Island will remember Mr. Pritam Singh Rangar, head teacher at the Aga Khan Primary School for a long time to come.

He is going to the United Kingdom for further studies after his stay of nearly three years in Mafia.

He was given a farewell party by the pupils of the school, youngsters of the town and the members of the school committee. Presenting him with a cheque for £80 the manager, Mr. Abdul G. Rawji said that it was very rare to come across a sincere, efficient and a loyal teacher like Mr. Rangar who regarded the school children and the Ismalli Community as his own.

Before the Mafia assignment, Mr. Rangar was a graduate teacher at the Government High School, Bomdi-La, North East Frontier Agency, India.

He relocated to London, England in 1968 and took up teaching position with the Inner London Education Authority, teaching in various middle schools. He became actively involved within the community and participated in cultural and political events.

As part of the Indo-British Delegation he went to Gaza in Israel in 1994 where he met the PLO leader Yassar Arafat who expressed his great pleasure in meeting Pritam.

Pritam in dark blue blazer with Yasser Arafat of PLO-1994

COLONEL RUPINDER SINGH, CORPS OF ENGINEERS

Bomb Disposal

Specialist

Badge of Indian Army

Corps of Engineers

Rupinder, the third son of Sardarni Harbans Kaur, was commissioned in the Army Corps of Engineers in 1956. After graduating in Civil Engineering from the College of Military Engineering, he served on active duty field formations from Ladakh to Arunachal Pradesh (NEFA), Madhya Pradesh, Maharashtra, North Bengal, Upper Assam and Karnataka among other military stations in India. He raised a new engineer regiment at Sagar, Madhya Pradesh and moved the unit to North Bengal in support of an active Infantry Division. Later, he commanded an engineer regiment in upper Assam in support of Arunachal Pradesh theatre of operations. He commanded an Independent Bomb Disposal Unit in Delhi Cantonment for the protection of India's Capital City against enemy air raids.

After leaving army service in 1975, he went for higher studies abroad. He graduated with a degree in M.Ed. from the University of Bath, England, a degree in M.Eng. in Engineering from Memorial University of Newfoundland, Canada and another M.Eng. degree in Civil Engineering from the University of Alberta, Canada. He obtained his Doctorate in Engineering from Pacific Western University, USA.

Rupinder was employed with Newfoundland Oceans Research and Development Corporation from 1979 to 1982 as Head of Special Projects. The research projects were related to oceanographic data collection of cold waters of North Atlantic Ocean and fisheries economics assisting fish processing units in their marketing endeavours. He developed a simulation model for fisheries economics and presented this technical paper at the Sixth International Cost Engineering Congress in 1979 at Mexico City, Mexico. He later presented a paper at Fisherman's Forum at Bangor, Maine, USA.

While employed with Loram International, Calgary, Alberta, Canada, he presented technical papers at American Association of Cost Engineering forums in Philadelphia, USA and in Toronto, Canada. He was an adjunct professor with the University of Calgary, Alberta, Canada where he conducted management courses for graduate students and local senior corporate management.

| Conducted Management Seminars, Canada 1981 – 1984 | Technical Paper, Mexico City 1980 | Technical Paper, Philadelphia, USA |

M.Eng. Civil Canada

M.Eng. Engineering

Memorial University of Newfoundland, Canada

M.Ed. England

Ph.D. USA

Certified Cost Engineer, American Association of Cost Engineers, USA

He operated as President of an engineering consulting firm in the San Francisco Bay Area for over 14 years prior to his retirement. He is settled in the San Francisco Bay Area, California, USA, since 1986.

SURINDER KAUR SAHNEY, B.A., B.ED. WITH HER HUSBAND BRIGADIER SARANJIT SINGH SAHNEY

After the partition of India in 1947, the family was uprooted from Multan and finally settled down in the princely State of Patiala. Her parents had provided her good early education and so with this background, she was easily accepted in the Modern School at Patiala where she continued her education and passed the Matriculation examination of Panjab University in 1955 with a First division standing. Besides her academic excellence, she took a keen interest in extra-curricular activities such as drama, music and singing, winning several awards. She was recognised as the best singer in the school.

She joined the Government College for Woman in Patials, passed the Intermediate Examination (Faculty of Arts) and continued her studies at Mahendra College, Patiala graduating with a Bachelors degree. She represented the college in youth festival in dramatics winning the Silver Medal and she was adjudged the best singer. She also took active interest in National Cadet Corps (NCC) and enjoyed being a team player.

After graduating from Mahendra College, she continued her studies in the field of education joining the State College of Education in 1959 successfully completing the degree of Bachelor of Education (B.Ed.). During this educational program, she joined Girls Guide programme and actively participated in other on campus activities.

She was married to an Army Officer (Saranjit Singh Sahney) in 1960 who later retired as a Brigadier in the Army Corps of Signals. During her husband's military tenure he was posted to several army stations and Surrender would take keen interest in the welfare of army wives and started nursery schools for the regimental families.

Her family of one son and two daughters grew up exceptionally well. Her son joined the Army and completed prestigious service courses including the Long Gunnery Course at the School of Artillery at Deolali in Maharashtra standing first in the class and was recipient of the Silver Gun in recognition of this. He rose to the rank of Colonel and died unexpectedly with a medical emergency. Her elder daughter has a Ph.D. in psychology and is well settled. Her younger daughter is a computer specialist settled in USA.

With her keen interest in cooking, she published a book on cookery that she dedicated to her mother.

After her husband's retirement, she is now settled in Chandigarh.

COLONEL DEVINDER SINGH

Badge of Corps of Electrical

and Mechanical Engineers

Devinder, born in Multan, now in Pakistan, was six years old at the time of the partition of India in 1947. His pre-school education was suddenly disrupted and he moved with the uprooted family along with his mother Sardarni Harbans Kaur to various destinations.

During his early years of education, Devinder showed a natural instinct in science and technology. On joining college, he enrolled in science subjects and mathematics. Later, after successfully passing the Union Public Services Commission competitive examination followed by selection at the Services Selection Board assessment in Meerut, Uttar Pradesh, he joined the Indian Military Academy in Dehra Dun, Uttranchal Pradesh. He was granted a permanent regular commission in the Corps of Electrical and Mechanical branch of the Army in 1963 as per his choice.

He completed his engineering degree from the College of Military Engineering, Dapodi, Maharashtra and continued his further education at the Military College of Electronics and Mechanical Engineering at Secunderabad, Andhra Pradesh. The role of Corps of Electrical and Mechanical Engineers (EME) is to achieve and maintain the operational fitness of electrical, mechanical, electronics and optical equipment of the Army.

As an EME officer, he maintained everything the Army used. With forward repair teams his responsibility within the operational area was in recovering equipment casualties from their place of damage. His postings were at many military workshops across India. His first posting was to Mumbai where he was assigned the responsibility of inspection of Mahindra & Mahindra jeeps prior to their induction into the Army. While posted as a workshop officer at Bhopal, Madhya Pradesh, he enriched his interest in world history by completing his M.A. degree from Panjabi University, Patiala, Punjab.

Panjabi University, Patiala, Punjab

Among other assignments across many army stations, he was entrusted with his challenging command of a workshop in J&K during 1965 war with Pakistan. During this active duty assignment in war zone in Jammu & Kashmir, he provided repair and maintenance support to field artillery and armoured units in Haji Pir Pass. Besides his technical responsibilities in repair and maintenance of guns and armour, he also participated in active infantry patrols in Baramula sector of Kashmir valley. Incidentally, Sardarni Harbans Kaur visited her son during the period of active hostilities in Baramula Sector of J&K and accompanied him right up to the border area in Ranjit Singh Pura Sector.

Devinder took premature retirement from the army service after completing meritorious service in 1987 and relocated to Mississauga, Ontario, Canada. Here, he started a successful computer sales and repair business that he named after his father called "Nanak Computers." Additionally he became a real estate and mortgage broker and joined a progressive real estate company in Toronto, Canada.

COLONEL KULVINDER SINGH, PSC, LGSC

Defence Services Staff

College

Badge of Regiment of

Artillery

Sardarni Harbans Kaur had ingrained in all her children to strive for excellence in whatever they plan to do in life. In College, he joined National Cadet Corps (NCC) where he had a rapid rise to be an Under Officer Later he joined the Indian Military Academy, Dehra Dun, Uttaranchal.

All through his military service career, Kulvinder has been a very bright officer in the Regiment of Artillery. He commanded field batteries of heavy mortars and field guns. He completed two of the most prestigious courses in the Army viz Long Gunnery Staff Course (LGSC) and the Defence Services Staff Course (psc).

He served in high altitude areas of Ladakh, Bomdi-La in Arunachal Pradesh (China Tibet Border) and later he led a Battery of Heavy Mortars in the Jaisalmer and Barmer Sectors in Rajasthan during Indo-Pakistan was of 1971. He fired heavy mortars on the advancing enemy tanks and soldiers hiding behind sand dunes. The combined effort of his Artillery support in coordination with Armor and close support by the Indian Air Force, achieved a decisive victory in the Western Sector where entire Pakistani advancing tank brigade was neutralised. His continuation in service would have advanced him to the higher echelons of the army as a General in the Army.

Kulvinder at present is running a very successful Real Estate and Mortgage Brokerage business in Toronto, Canada.

WING COMMANDER BRIJINDER SINGH
(1945-1985)

Badge of Indian Air Force

The younger son Brijinder, maintained an exceptionally brilliant academic record. His early education was in a private public school where he completed his Matriculation examination maintaining first division. Later he joined Mahendra College, Patiala for his Faculty of Arts and Bachelor of Arts degrees majoring in Geography and Economics. During his college days he took part in student debates and remained an active member of the student union.

Following the footsteps of his four older brothers, he too desired to join the defence services. He took the competitive examinations of the All India Union Public Services Commission examinations for commissioning in the Indian Army as well as the Indian Air Force. Impressively, he qualified for both, a rare accomplishment. He opted for the Air Force and after successfully completing his initial training at the Air Force Academy at Coimbatore in Southern Indian State of Tamil Nadu, he was commissioned as a Pilot Officer. Due to his good professional performance he rose to the rank of Wing Commander.

Brijinder too had the linguistic gift and successfully completed the two year-long interpreter course in the Russian Language with distinction from the School of Foreign Languages, Government of India. Because of his excellent verbal and written skills, he was retained at the Air Headquarters in New Delhi to interpret and translate confidential/secret documents written in the Russian language that were being received by the Ministry of Defence, Government of India in the early eighties.

Brijinder was progressing well in his career with a bright future, but we lost him in 1985 at the young age of forty. He has left behind one daughter and one son who are both senior professionals settled in California, USA.

DR. RAMI RANGER, CBE, FRSA

The youngest son, Raminder Singh, popularly known as Rami Ranger, was born posthumously in 1947 in Gujranwala, now in Pakistan. The family moved to Ferozepur and finally to the State of Patiala in 1948. His schooling up to matriculation was in Patiala. After completing his B.A. degree from Panjab University, Chandigarh, he moved to London in 1968 with £5 in his pocket. His elder brother Pritam, who was already settled in London provided the initial support for a few months. With his entrepreneurial skills, he made a few changes in his initial jobs and finally established his own business enterprise under the name of Sun Mark, Limited. The growth of this business under his leadership is simply phenomenal. He exports his products to well over 82 countries worldwide. The export volume is among the highest in the United Kingdom. In recognition of his outstanding achievements, he has been awarded the Queen's Awards for Exports for five consecutive years - a rare achievement. The 2015 awards was presented personally by Honourable David Cameron, Prime Minister of the United Kingdom.

Five Consecutive Queen's Awards

Man of the Year Award

CBE awarded by Her Majesty,

the Queen in 2016

Rami became a Member of the British Empire (MBE) at an investure ceremony by His Highness Prince Charles in 2005. He also had an audience with Her Majesty, the United Kingdom & Dominions. He holds a Doctorate degree to his credit. Recently, he has published an autobiography *From Nothing to Everything* by a publisher in the United Kingdom. In 2016, he was awarded the coveted honour The Commander of the British Empire medal for his outstanding achievements in business.

MBE Awarded by HRH Prince Charles 2005

An audience with Her Majesty, the Queen of England

After his very successful business growth, he wanted to give back to the community. In this desire, he donated a substantial monetary gift to London South Bank University for their Centre for Graduate Entrepreneurship that is named after him.

Rami with Rt. Hon Theresa Villiers MP

Dr Rami Ranger Centre for Graduate Entrepreneurship at London South Bank University